THE QUILT DIGEST

THE QUILT DIGEST PRESS   SAN FRANCISCO   3

THE QUILT DIGEST

ISBN 0-913327-02-6
ISSN 0740-4093
Library of Congress Catalog Card Number: 82-90743
Printed on 100 lb. Satin Kinfuji and 260g/m² Bon Ivory (cover) by
Nissha Printing Company, Ltd., Kyoto, Japan.
Color separations by the printer.

Edited by Michael M. Kile.
Book design by Jeanne Jambu in association with Linda Lane and Kristin Marx Meuser,
Kajun Graphics, San Francisco.
Typographical composition in Sabon by Rock & Jones, San Francisco.
Editing assistance provided by Harold Nadel, San Francisco.
Photographs not specifically credited were taken by Sharon Risedorph
and Lynn Kellner, San Francisco.

The Quilt Digest Press
955 Fourteenth Street
San Francisco 94114

CONTENTS

Once Out of Time

THE COLLECTOR

*by
Lacy
Folmar
Bullard*

*I*t is impossible to trace the path of Charleston's history in her quilts. Too much happened in the two centuries during which the tiny English settlement on the low Carolina coast became successively the leading city of Colonial America, an urbane center of wealth and culture in the post-Revolutionary United States and a scene of ruin and desolation following the social and economic upheaval known variously as the Civil War, the War Between the States or "the late unpleasantness." Still, the quilts left to us do tell a story.

These are not strictly quilts made in Charleston. "Low-country quilts" is probably a more accurate designation for those remain-

*All photographs
by Sharon Risedorph*

ing in the city today. In the social order of an earlier time, members of the planter aristocracy often had several plantations—John Drayton, builder of stately Drayton Hall up the Ashley River, once owned a princely thirty-one—plus a house in Charleston for the social season. The families moved between their residences; thus quilts from Pendleton, Chester, Liberty Hill, Blackville, Beaufort and Summerville are in the Charleston Museum collection. In most cases, little is known of the route by which they came to Charleston, but they are certainly a part of the local quilting tradition. And it is just this distinct local tradition that makes the Charleston Museum quilt collection so valuable.

Other museum collections around the country are larger; a fair number hold rarer individual examples. The uniqueness of the Charleston Museum quilts, especially those made before the last quarter of the nineteenth century, lies in their kinship, their identity with place and region and with a style of life which occurred here once out of time, then vanished forever.

The kinship of many of the quilts is evident in the very fabrics from which they are made. If we knew verifiable dates for all the quilts in the collection, we could produce an inventory of local fabric merchants' shelves for a given year. The same chintz print shows up in a number of quilts by one or several makers: in ambitious undertakings like a Broderie Perse coverlet or in a single album square. Sometimes these are easy to spot, like the medallions and wreaths printed to be used as cutouts for appliqué work. At other times, a single blossom or bird from a width of fabric is combined with other design elements in one quilt, then the same fabric is used as a whole-cloth border in another quilt.

Yet more than fabric connects these quilts. They seem to possess a mannered elegance and charm that sets them apart, as a group, from quilts made in other parts of the country. The best of them reflect the unique quality of life among the low-country elite of the period, those who, strongly influenced by English fashion, set the style and tone of Charleston society.

Charleston dates its founding from English settlers arriving in 1670, but no quilts or bedcoverings of the seventeenth-century colonists are known to survive. Examples from the eighteenth century are rare, and often only fragments. An eighteenth-century *palampore* with the East India Trading Company stamp still visible is owned by the Museum, but there is no documentation tying it to Charleston. No doubt others like it were among the imports that poured into this country during that century, coming at first by way of England and the Continent. Charleston as an important seaport would have received a large share of such imports, and wealth to keep them in the city surely was not wanting. An

eighteenth-century quilted fabric serves as a drapery in the 1828 Edmonston-Alston House owned by the Historic Charleston Foundation. It was originally part of a set of English bed hangings, probably imported when they were new.

There are various theories to explain the scarcity of eighteenth-century examples among low-country quilts. Laurel Horton, of the University of South Carolina's McKissick Museums at Columbia, is engaged in a study project on South Carolina quilts begun in 1983. She has done similar work on the quilts of North Carolina, and is of the opinion that few scrap or pieced quilts were made in these areas before the middle of the nineteenth century. She reasons that weaving was an easier and cheaper way to produce blankets and coverlets. Fabric suitable for making pieced quilts was in short supply locally, since homespun did not lend itself to piecing, and over much of the Carolinas it was the fabric most commonly in use.

Certainly her theory holds true for the majority of the populace, especially those living outside large cities, and among lower income groups. However, the planters and other wealthy Charlestonians could afford to do as they liked about such matters as bedcoverings. They would have liked, above all, to do what was fashionable—and that meant English fashion.

In *Patchwork,* Averil Colby points out that toward the end of the eighteenth century, there occurred in England what she terms a "noticeable crystallising of ideas and fashion in patchwork designs." [1] (The English refer to appliqué as patchwork.) Appliqué work had taken the place of embroidery; the most common design for quilts was a central panel framed by a series of borders; all-over pieced patterns like the *Honeycomb* of joined hexagons were broken up and came to be arranged in groups of "flowers" or in strips or borders as part of an overall composition. [2]

Quilts done in appliqué work, especially chintz florals, became widely popular and remained so into the second quarter of the nineteenth century, though such work, Colby admits, was typical "of the manor-house rather than the cottage." [3] These quilts gradually gave way to those made chiefly of pieced work, using the smaller-patterned cottons which were becoming readily available.

Some vestiges of the floral appliqués remain, however, in quilts designed for many years after, where the appliqué was almost always combined with pieced work.

In a general way, quiltmaking in Charleston followed these trends, if allowance is made for the time lag as fashion made the sea voyage from England, as well as for the time necessary to complete intricate examples of needlework for which South Carolina women must have collected fabrics over a period of many years. Here, as in England, the production of these elaborate bedcoverings was chiefly confined to the "manor-house" which, in the low country, meant the plantations.

Trapunto and corded quilting were major design elements in English bedcoverings. One quilt (page 9) in the Museum collection provides ample proof that these were popular also in fashion-conscious Charleston. An overall clamshell pattern in the off-white background is corded, surrounding the "flowers" pieced of hexagons which are appliquéd to the ground cloth. The small pieces are cut carefully from deliberately chosen small-scale prints and placed so that the printed fabrics make their own designs within the larger flower. Touches of chintz appliqué also appear on this quilt, which is dated circa 1829.

It might have been made in either Beaufort or Charleston, for 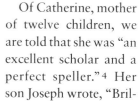 we know the quilter's name, and she lived in both places. Catherine Osborn Barnwell was born in Beaufort in 1809, but lived for some twenty years in Charleston, where her husband was the rector of St. Peter's Church before ill health forced his retirement to his Laurel Bay Plantation near Beaufort.

Of Catherine, mother of twelve children, we are told that she was "an excellent scholar and a perfect speller."[4] Her son Joseph wrote, "Brilliant and distinguished in conversation she never was, but she had wisdom which came to the aid of her deep religious conviction in the trying scenes of a life which extended to seventy-seven years."[5] Many of those "trying scenes" must have occurred when she, with the help of one of her sons, was left to run Laurel Bay in 1857 while her husband went north for medical treatment. The ensuing war, which disrupted most travel, prevented his return, and he died

in Pennsylvania, separated from home and family, never to see Catherine or Laurel Bay again.

An undocumented story comes with the quilt to the effect that the corded clamshells, or perhaps the insertion of the cording, was done by slaves—or "servants," as the Charlestonians preferred to call them. Perhaps. Mrs. Barnwell undoubtedly had slaves; no plantation ran without them. Yet the story may well be no more than a latter-day explanation for a task which seems to modern eyes so tedious that only someone who had no choice would undertake it.

In addition to her reputed spelling prowess and her obvious talents in needlework, Catherine Barnwell is said to have loved gardening. That would not be surprising in Charleston, then or now. The English love of gardening was, if anything, heightened among the settlers with leisure to pursue it, who found themselves among new plants in a new coun-

try. Dr. Alexander Garden was an eighteenth-century Scottish physician and botanist who lived in Charleston and whose name is commemorated by the genus *Gardenia*. The botanical Bartrams of Philadelphia, John and his son William, knew Charleston. John counted among his correspondents the aristocratic Elizabeth Lamboll, who communicated (through her husband, as was proper) information on what she grew in her notable garden, and from time to time supplied native plants to the naturalist until his death in 1777.[6] A Lamboll daughter had a similar association with William some two decades later, though by then it seems to have been proper to correspond directly instead of through a third party.[7]

We do not know that Catherine Barnwell had any such claims to gardening fame, or if Elizabeth Lamboll had any talent for quilt-making. It seems likely, however,

that many Charleston women may have combined the two interests; after all, gardening was a fashionable English pastime. Indeed, Charleston architects, designers and ironworkers were just as fashion-conscious: floral motifs are lavishly depicted in Charleston architecture and ironwork (page 10 and this page).

Because of the gardening passion and breakthroughs in fabric printing, the first fifteen years or so of the nineteenth century saw a great boom in the production of fabrics with floral designs made

specifically to be cut out and appliquéd in the Broderie Perse style of needlework. Centers, borders and garlands show up time and again in quilts from the first half of the century, and Charleston quilters certainly used their share.

A floral bouquet wreathed in a flowery vine is appliquéd at the center of a very large (125 × 124 inches) quilt of fine cambric (above); birds, butterflies and sprigs of flowers are placed symmetrically on the surrounding fabric. Bouquets in vases appear at the four corners of the central section, and a landscape medallion is centered on each side and at the top and the bottom. Some of these appliqués, including the landscape medallions, are identical with those used on two other quilts of the same date which were given to the Museum by another donor. In their time, such fabrics were probably the latest craze in Charleston, eagerly sought after and skillfully used by many of the finest quiltmakers.

This quilt, shown here on an eighteenth-century mahogany poster bed in the 1772 Heyward-Washington House which belongs to the Museum, has a wide chintz inner border, its color and glaze still bright and glowing. An outer border, also of chintz, is more fragile and faded. Fine quilting secures the top to the cambric backing, and holds the thin batting in place. The edge is finished with a tape binding.

Daniel Heyward built this house on Church Street, and his son Thomas, a signer of the Declaration of Independence (one of four from Charleston), lived here until 1794. The house acquired its second name because it was rented as quarters for President Washington during his visit to Charleston in 1791. The bed has come down through the family, and came to the Museum from them.

Also shown on this bed is an unlined spread (at right) which must have few equals anywhere for the amount, detail and intricacy of its appliqué. It measures 118 × 108 inches, and the white cotton background fabric is appliquéd overall in chintz cutouts arranged in the *Flowering Tree* pattern. The many fabrics used in constructing the piece date from 1815 to approximately 1830. There is no backing or batting, and the wide floral chintz border is unhemmed.

Maria Bord Schulz, a native Charlestonian born in 1806, made this spread, which takes its inspiration from the eighteenth-century Indian *palampores* like the one in the Museum's collection. She skillfully formed the landscape from

which the tree rises by overlaying sections of fabric to represent small hills and rocky outcrops. These are dotted with trees, flowers, Oriental teahouses and pagodas, mounted hunters and their prey, groups of serenely contemplative Orientals, even a whimsical — if incongruous — giraffe (below). The composition of the tree with its fantastic birds and blossoms fills the remaining space. The chintz in the border is the same as that used in the border of a pieced star quilt in the collection which dates from the early nineteenth century.

By the middle of the nineteenth century in England, pieced work, often of silk and velvet, had largely replaced chintz appliqué as the handwork of manor-house ladies who set needlework fashion. Perhaps chintz appliqué lingered longer in the low country because of the popularity of friendship and album quilts. These were often made from squares of muslin appliquéd with chintz flowers and birds. Frequently, each square was signed, and sometimes conveniently dated, by its maker. These squares might be set together as soon as they were made, particularly if the quilt was meant to be a gift for a wedding or other special occasion. In other cases, the finished squares languished, safely but out of sight, among family treasures until they

might become a quilt at last, thanks to some sentimental descendant. The Charleston Museum has several sets of such blocks, carefully wrapped and saved still, as they must have been for decades in some Charleston attic.

In an era of uncomfortable transportation, roomy houses and plenty of servants, lengthy visits were the rule, sometimes extending over months. Groups of relatives and friends thus gathered would often turn to quiltmaking as a pleasant and suitable diversion, producing lovely and lasting souvenirs. Squares for album quilts might also be exchanged by mail among quilting friends and family.

An album quilt (at left) owned by the Historic Charleston Foundation is shown on an eighteenth-century mahogany poster bed of New York manufacture in the Foundation's 1808 Nathaniel Russell House on Meeting Street. One square, signed "Jane Windsor, Charleston," is dated 1844, and another reads "Martha K. Martin,

Augusta, Ga. 1842." On the back is sewn a label, "Elizabeth Cordes from Grandmother," with the date either 1851 or 1857. This quilt is interesting for its rather uncommon diagonal setting of the squares, with strips made of a narrow floral striped chintz in two different background colors, one sky blue, the other cream.

Inside the Joseph Manigault House (above), built in 1803 and designed for his brother by Charleston's first "gentleman-

architect," Gabriel Manigault, can be found a Charleston-made "rice bed," so called because the posts (at left) are carved with fruiting heads of the grain upon which so many Charleston fortunes were based. The Manigaults themselves were wealthy rice planters, and this house, now a Museum property, with its small gate temple through which guests enter the grounds (inset), is like a distant reflection of their way of life.

The spread (page 16) pictured on the rice bed has no connection with the Manigaults, so far as we know, but was made in Charleston and Blackville in 1847 and 1848. Its thirty-six squares are set together and bordered by strips of boldly printed floral chintz. Fifteen of the squares bear signatures of family members and friends of Claudia L. Chapman of Blackville, whose daughter donated this quilt to the Museum. The square done predominantly in blues (page 16) is signed "Mrs R Kirkland Blackville 1848." The other (page 16)

reads "Harriet Blackwood Charleston," who apparently was not sure whether the date was for starting or finishing: she changed her 1847 to 1848. Claudia Chapman herself signed two of the squares. This spread is unlined but bound with tape. Such spreads were often called "summer throws" and would have been useful in the warm, humid low-country climate.

The quilt on this page represents a complete break with the chintz tradition, and is more akin to the pieced work of velvet and silk popular in England in the year it was made, 1852. Paths of navy hexagons delineate the stars and diamonds, also made up of hexagons, which form changing patterns as one looks at this carefully pieced quilt. Silk taffetas and

brocades in brilliant colors are used throughout, and the backing is gold silk with widely-spaced yellow stripes. A navy border is quilted in a cable design, then finished with a red and blue silk fringe. The quilt is the work of Marina Gregg, wife of Charleston silversmith William Gregg. It earned her the award for Best Quilt from the Southern Central Agricultural Society Exposition, probably in the year it was made. And it shows that the English hexagon tradition was well-copied in the Charleston area.

Another example of beautifully executed hexagonal patchwork is the fragment (at left) made up of seven stars formed from extremely small pieces and showing clever use of printed and plain fabrics to work out the design. All we know about this piece is that it was "made by the donor's great-grandmother Baldwin at Box's Plantation on the North May River."[8]

More low-country quilts from the nineteenth century survive than are included in the Charleston

Museum collection. A few belong to other public institutions in the city, and a few others remain in private hands, passed down within local families. Some of the finest examples, however, are no longer in Charleston; other museums guard the treasures now. In the way that an aristocratic lady down on her luck might part with heirloom jewelry, Charleston saw many of her quilts sold to private collectors, institutions and museums with large endowments in the early years of this century. Charleston's economy was not booming at that period, true, but the same gathering-up was taking place across the country. The idea of regional arts and crafts did not have the importance it would later assume, and knowing collectors could pick and choose. Many museums around the country prize their South Carolina quilts.

Charleston's fine old buildings were being stripped of their ornamentation or torn down for their materials during the same period, before public indignation finally was aroused, and the "artistic vandalism" was stopped. Among those not content to see the city's treasures bought and carried away was Miss Laura Bragg. She had come to Charleston as an assistant to the director of the Museum, in charge of the library and educational activities, then became its director in 1920. Since its founding in 1773, the Museum, proud to have the "oldest established museum collection in North America," had been devoted primarily to natural history. Under its new director, it began to enlarge its field of interest. Laura Bragg realized the value of the elegant furnishings and decorative arts that had been so much a part of the area's colorful history. She actively sought and secured for the Museum all the examples she could. Through her efforts, the first quilts were gathered.

The Museum had been rechartered as an institution separate from the College of Charleston in 1915, but suffered through the years from lack of space and facilities. After moving through a series of temporary and inadequate locations, a much-needed permanent home was funded by a city-county bond issue and completed in 1980. A few months later the old Thompson Auditorium, which had been home to the Museum for many years prior to the last move, burned to the ground. By such a small margin did the quilt collection survive to be installed in its safe new quarters.

As the Museum's personnel can attest, adequate funding is always a problem, but many Charlestonians seem aware that in their quilts they possess a rare collection of documented social history, rich for its distinct local tradition. There is much left to document, preserve and add to the collection, but a start has been made. It is generally agreed that Charleston's greatest contribution to the arts in America is in the field of architecture, so the motto on her city seal is appropriate: "She guards her buildings, customs and law." Now, thanks to increasing public support, many dedicated staff members and volunteers at the Museum, she is adding her quilts to the list.

REFERENCE LIST

1. Averil Colby, *Patchwork* (Newton Centre, Massachusetts: Charles T. Branford, 1958; rpt. New York: Charles Scribner's Sons, 1982), p. 102.

2. *Ibid.*

3. *Ibid.,* p. 118.

4. Stephen B. Barnwell, *The Story of an American Family* (Marquette, Michigan: self-published, 1969), p. 119.

5. *Ibid.*

6. Elise Pinckney, *Thomas and Elizabeth Lamboll: Early Charleston Gardeners* (Charleston: Charleston Museum, November 1969), p. v.

7. *Ibid.,* pp. 37–39.

8. From a Charleston Museum registry card documenting this fragment.

LACY FOLMAR BULLARD is a free-lance writer and editor living in Tallahassee, Florida. Here she combines two favorite subjects, antique quilts and Charleston. Long a Charleston Museum enthusiast, she studied its quilt collection in 1982 while doing research for *Chintz Quilts: Unfading Glory,* written with Betty Jo Shiell and published by Serendipity Publishers.

By Patricia T. Herr

*T*he quilts of America's minority religious sects fascinate quilt enthusiasts. The examples of Amish and Mennonite needlework fairly leap to mind. And the creations of other groups, such as the Dunkards, have been collected and admired regionally for a number of years. Much of the attention paid such quilts derives not only from design qualities peculiar to their type, but also from an avid interest in the people who made them. A good-sized room could be filled, for example, by the articles, pamphlets and books written about the Amish and Mennonites during the past decade.

Yet this interest does not seem to extend to the Quakers and their quilts. It may be that the Quakers' successful assimilation into the daily routine of American life accounts for this disinterest. Or it may be the complete lack of documentation and discussion of this definable group of quilts that is to blame.

To appreciate Quaker quilts fully, one must first have some understanding of the people who made and used them. Conversely, as we study their material objects, such as quilts, we can come to understand better the people, their culture and their times.

The Quakers, more properly called the Religious Society of Friends, were organized as a group in the mid-1600's by George Fox, an Englishman. In Fox's own words, the name "Quaker" came into use in this way: "This Justice Bennet of Darby, who was the first that called us Quakers, because I bid them tremble at the word of the Lord. And this was in the year 1650." [1]

The Friends first came to the American Colonies in 1656, when they held Meetings for Worship in Rhode Island, Massachusetts and Maryland. Theirs was a pyramidal lay organization that had no paid clergy and divided its Meetings into small Preparative (weekly or twice-weekly) and Monthly gatherings, larger county-wide Quarterly Meetings and Yearly Meetings that served as regional conferences.

In the religious context, women Friends were on an almost equal footing with men. For example, in 1681, at the first Yearly Meeting of East and West Jersey in Burlington, New Jersey, it was agreed to hold women's business meetings at the same time as men's. [2] Separate business meetings were widely instituted to ensure that women, less likely to voice strong opinions in front of their husbands, brothers or fathers, would engage in serious discussion. Women could speak regarding a problem, such as regulating marriages, controlling school funds or disciplining and disowning members; but, in both the women's and men's sessions, the "weighty" members (frequently those of financial substance) had the greatest influence. Although women had no power to disown their members and had to rely on the men's meetings for financial support, they could preach, serve as elders and overseers and publish religious writings of their own. Some women even traveled to distant Meetings to preach to other Friends. [3]

By the end of the seventeenth century, Quaker society reached down most of the Atlantic seaboard with Meetings scattered throughout Rhode Island, Massachusetts, New York, Pennsylvania, Maryland, Virginia and North Carolina. Within these

All in Modesty

Quilting at the Westown Friends School, 1906. Photograph courtesy of Chester County Historical Society, West Chester, Pennsylvania. □

and Plainness

growing, prospering communities, quilts would have been created in quantity, along with other household items. Yet, as with these other decorative arts, few textiles of the late seventeenth century survive; there are, for example, no documented Quaker quilts of this period.

The Philadelphia Museum of Art, however, is fortunate to have in its collection a quilt (this page) that was owned by Elizabeth Coates Paschall (1702–1767). This first-generation American Quaker personifies the well-to-do Delaware Valley Quaker woman during this early settlement period. She was the daughter of Philadelphia merchant Thomas Coates, who emigrated from England in 1686, and Beulah Jacquette, of French origin. In 1721, Elizabeth married another prominent Philadelphian, Joseph Paschall, and nine children were born to this marriage.[4] After her husband's death in 1742, Elizabeth Paschall continued to be active, purchasing land that had been in the Coates family. On this acreage she erected Cedar Grove, which passed to her relations, the socially-prominent Morris family; it is situated in what is now Fairmont Park in Philadelphia. She and her sister-in-law, Mary Coates, also bought in partnership fabric yardage for speculation and resale.[5]

Although Elizabeth's activities were unusual for a woman of her time, she was in a position financially and socially to be able to pursue these interests. It is not likely that poorer women Friends could follow such a course, as they would be burdened with the

Whole-cloth, owned and possibly made by Elizabeth Coates Paschall, Philadelphia, first half of the eighteenth century, 101 × 102 inches, silk. Collection of the Philadelphia Museum of Art (Bequest of Lydia Thompson Morris). □

Detail of back, printed cotton, probably imported from India. □

everyday duties of the household, the family and child care. Except for a few prominent eighteenth-century women Friends, the majority of Quaker women had no more freedom in their secular lives than did their non-Quaker counterparts.

It is likely that Elizabeth Coates Paschall, with the help of her friends, made this quilt. In a journal of another, slightly later Quaker, Elizabeth Drinker, there is this entry, made before her marriage to Henry Drinker: "Nov. 20 1758 Took a walk in ye morning to Sarah Plumly's; called at Uncles, at C. Nicholdson's, and at C. Richardson's and at J. Richardson's. Dined and spent ye afternoon at Betsy Moodes's, helped to quilt. Spent ye evening at F. Rawles."[6] From such journals and diaries, it appears that young women in these aristocratic Quaker families spent their time not doing housework, but visiting other Friends, dining out, traveling and socializing. In her journal, Elizabeth Drinker frequently mentions time spent sewing and doing needlework.

Since Elizabeth Coates Paschall was born in America, it is likely that her quilt was made on this side of the Atlantic. Researchers in England concerned with the export of British textiles into America in the eighteenth century have yet to find references to quilts being shipped at that time, although large amounts of fabrics were being sent in.[7] Although there is strong evidence that the quilt was made in America, it resembles English quilts. Plain silk quilts of this type can be found in the British Isles.[8]

They were popular in England until the beginning of the nineteenth century.[9] In America the Quakers continued this tradition well into the nineteenth century.

Because of the close association the wealthy Quaker merchants had with overseas trade—in particular, the British East India Company—expensive and fashionable imported Chinese silk fabrics were accessible to them. Shipping records of the British East India Company from 1721 through 1824 indicate orders of both plain and patterned silks from Canton. From specifications for these fabrics supplied by the company, it has been possible to identify some Quaker dresses as having been made from imported Chinese silk.[10]

It is interesting to note this entry in Elizabeth's cousin Samuel Coates's account book: "Joseph Paschall [Elizabeth's husband] 7mo 23, 1732 to 1# silk @ 40/ 5-2-0."[11] This indicates that Elizabeth indeed did have fabric on hand to produce such a piece.

The top of this bedcovering relies solely on the elegant quilting with fine silk thread for its ornamentation. The central motif is a floral medallion surrounded by an inner border of clamshell quilting and finished with an outer border of flower-tipped plumes. Background areas are filled with diamond quilting. The contrasting, vivid cotton back (page 24), probably printed in India, enhances the subtleties of the silk top.

The quilt exemplifies Quaker attitudes toward decorative arts and furnishings of the time. These can be summarized by the oft-quoted phrase "of the best Sort, but Plain."[12] Frederick B. Tolles, a modern Quaker historian, has suggested that "Wives and daughters of the Quaker Grandees compensated for their self-denial in the matter of ornaments by having their garments made only of the finest and most expensive stuffs."[13] Contemporary observers of the early Quakers made similar comments. In 1724, Christopher Sauer, the Pennsylvania German printer, observed that plainness was still notable in Quaker garb, "except that the material is very costly, or is even velvet."[14] Twenty-six years later, Swedish traveler Peter Kalm attended a Friends Meeting and noted that although Quakers "pretend not to have their clothes made after the latest fashion, or to wear cuffs and be dressed as gaily as others, they strangely enough have their garments made of the finest and costliest materials that can be procured."[15]

As the Delaware Valley Friends became affluent, the trappings of their wealth drew them away from the simple Quaker way of life. Continually through the history of Quaker settlement in America, "weighty" members made statements in Yearly Meeting Minutes admonishing Friends to adhere to the basic Quaker principles of "equality, simplicity, and peace."[16] Particularly in this pre-Revolutionary period, one can see the stress under which the wealthy Quaker merchant families must have lived. By adhering to the very virtues that were basic to Quakerism, these businessmen flourished

Sunburst, *by
Rebecca Scattergood
Savery, Philadelphia,
1839, 119 1/2 × 115
inches, pieced cotton
chintzes. Collection
of the Philadelphia
Museum of Art (Gift
of Sarah Pennell
[Mrs. Lewis] Barton
and Nancy Barton
[Mrs. David]
Barclay).* □

and achieved great wealth and social status. They truly became the "merchant princes" of the New World.

Nevertheless, frequent warnings fundamental to Quaker doctrine had been issued as early as 1667 by founder George Fox: "Keep out of the vain fashion of the World....Therefore, keep all in modesty and plainness."[17] Minutes of the 1695 Philadelphia Yearly Meeting urged Friends to "Keep to Plainness in Apparell" and "all be Careful about Making, Buying or Wearing (as much as they can) Striped or Flower'd Stuffs, or other useless & Superfluous Things."[18] □

With this moral dilemma in mind, consider the quilt (page 26) made by Rebecca Scattergood Savery for her first granddaughter, Sarah Savery, in 1839. The top is pieced from diamonds of elegant cotton chintzes in a *Sunburst* of riotous color. The interlining is cotton batting, and the back is an equally elegant roller-printed cotton chintz showing exotic foliage of more subdued brown hues. Rebecca chose her fabrics to include thirty-four of the finest, most elaborate imported chintzes available at that time. There appears to have been no effort on her part to make a "plain" quilt devoid of "Flower'd Stuffs."

Rebecca, who lived from 1770 to 1855, married Thomas, son of the renowned Philadelphia cabinetmaker William Savery. Thomas played a prominent role in Philadelphia Quaker affairs and was an elder in the Arch Street Friends Meeting. So, as the Savery men, Quakers though they may have been, were producing some of the most ornamental of Philadelphia furniture, an equally stylish quilt was being made by one of the Savery women.

During the Revolutionary period, the Friends were forced by their pacifist beliefs to withdraw from the political scene. Among members of the sect a reaction against excessive accommodation to "the world" followed, and in 1777 committees were formed to visit the membership and impress upon them the importance of plainness of speech, behavior, personal apparel and household furniture.[19] Quaker authority J. William Frost sums up the problem by saying that "Eighteenth-century Quakerism was caught between the ideal of reforming the world and the desire to escape from the world to build a holy community. Generally, Quakers decided to work to reform the world at the risk of some degree of contamination."[20] □

Although Quakers dominated the aristocratic classes of Philadelphia and Newport, Rhode Island, the majority of Friends were farmers and country people. Contemporaries distinguished between city and country Quakers as "wet" and "strict" Friends.[21] Rachel Taylor, who made the Center Square variation (page 28), was born and reared in the rural setting of Chester County, Pennsylvania. Her family were members of the Bradford Monthly Meeting. Rachel made this quilt in 1811, the year she married Quaker farmer William Lamborn. In the upper center she chain-stitched, with rust-colored wool, a cartouche containing her name and the date (page 28).

The quilt is all wool, including the interlining of unbleached, unspun wool. It is quilted with linen thread. It is interesting to note that the glazed blue plain-woven center and inner corner blocks are actually pieces of a petticoat cut up and recycled as a quilt. This blue wool is probably imported fabric; but the striped back of the petticoat, along with the several other backing materials, appears to be of domestic handspun and woven goods.

This is not the only Quaker quilt known to have been made from a petticoat. An all-silk Center Square quilt in the collection of the Chester County Historical Society has at its center a petticoat, taken off the waistband, then cut in two, with the top edges pieced together. It was made from the 1773 wedding dress of Mary Davis Ashbridge. In that year her marriage was recorded in the Chester Monthly Meeting, and she and her husband, Joshua, settled on their country homestead in Goshen, Chester County, Pennsylvania.[22] □

Center Square variation, by Rachel Taylor, Bradford Township, Chester County, Pennsylvania, 1811, 97 × 103 inches, pieced from a petticoat and other glazed wools. Collection of Eleanor Marshall Reynolds. □

Detail, showing maker's name and the date in a needlework cartouche. □

28

Elaborately quilted petticoats of the type that were remade into these quilts were in vogue in England from the 1750's to the 1770's and in America during the late eighteenth and early nineteenth centuries.[23] During this period the skirts of stylish dresses were of an "open robe" design, showing off the petticoat as a panel down the front. As this fashion became outmoded, the Quaker women, who particularly favored silk quilts, saw an opportunity to reuse their beautiful needlework in bedcoverings.

A petticoat (this page) thought to have been made in 1797 by a Quaker teacher, Ann Marsh, is also in the collection of the Chester County Historical Society. The outer fabric is pale blue plain-woven silk, and the lining is a darker blue plain-woven wool cloth. It is interlined with unspun, unbleached wool. (In England a number of petticoats contain blue-dyed, unspun wool,[24] an observation the author has made of American petticoats as well.)

Typical of these Quaker silk petticoats are the quilting patterns. Intricate, tightly quilted leaf and floral motifs are found at the bottom. The quilting, done with silk thread, is less dense toward the waistband, where the fabric was bunched together, unseen under the top of the dress skirt.

Ann Marsh, born in 1717 in Worcester, England, was a talented and prolific needlewoman, if one may judge by her surviving pieces in the Chester County Historical So-

BRIAN R. TOLBERT

Silk quilted petticoat, by Ann Marsh, Chester County, Pennsylvania, late eighteenth century. Collection of the Chester County Historical Society, West Chester, Pennsylvania. □

ciety and private collections. A variety of items, including a silk pincushion, a pair of wool-worked pockets, a needlework case of silk, a sampler, a wool-worked seat cushion and pillow and several needlework pictures are in these collections. Ann was not alone among Quaker women in doing her needlework. Many exquisite examples from the end of the eighteenth and early nineteenth centuries survive in the Westown Friends School and other public and private collections. Elizabeth Drinker, in her journal notations of 1758–1760,[25] prior to her marriage, makes reference to working on a quilt, petticoat and Bible cover.

The daughter of Joseph and Elizabeth Alebone Marsh, Ann emigrated to America

with her parents. Although she never married, she did teach the children of prominent Philadelphians in the 1770's and 1780's. She then retired to Chester County; she died there in 1797 and is believed buried in an unmarked grave in the Goshen or Willistown Friends Cemetery. Surviving Ann on the back of one of her embroidered pictures is this inscription:

Ann Marsh
her work
173[ ]
Oh time, time why dost Thou leave us this.
When she that wrought thy showy surface
Is mouldering into dust. □

Quaker women did not limit their quilting to primarily silk and wool fabrics. By the middle of the nineteenth century, as did other groups of women, the Friends were producing album and friendship quilts. These usually consisted of small-scale cotton prints with white cotton as a background. Although the Quaker quilts do not seem to attain the elaborate intricacy of those produced by the Baltimore Methodists, nor the free-wheeling, exuberant use of pattern and color found in the Pennsylvania German quilts of that period, they are consistently fine in their needlework and choice of fabric. They project a feeling of restrained elegance.

29

Detail of Oak Leaf *and* The Reel *variation corner block.* □

Friendship, 1850, Chester County, Pennsylvania, 95 × 90 inches, pieced and appliquéd cottons. Made for Enoch and Mary Worrall and signed by members of the Bradford Hicksite Meeting. Collection of Elizabeth and Philip Gibson. □

The quilt (this page) made in 1850 for Enoch and Mary Worrall, members of the Bradford (Chester County, Pennsylvania) Hicksite Quaker Meeting, is an example of the mid-nineteenth-century Quaker friendship quilt. Each block is signed in ink with the name of a different member or couple of that Meeting. At the time this quilt was made, the Worralls' children, whose names all appear on the quilt, ranged from eighteen to thirty-six years old. As seems to have been the custom at the time, the name of Phoebe, a deceased daughter, also appears on the family block.

The stars are precisely cut and sewn. Their backgrounds vary among white and tiny prints in a balanced layout. The only variations in this layout are the two bottom

Friendship, 1845–1849, Bucks County, Pennsylvania, 102 × 102 inches, pieced and appliquéd cottons. Signed by members of the Middletown Hicksite Meeting. Collection of Richard and Rosemarie Machmer.

□

Another example of a mid-nineteenth-century cotton Quaker friendship quilt (this page) comes from Bucks County, Pennsylvania. The colored fabrics are an assortment of diminutive prints pieced and appliquéd on a plain white cotton background. These blocks are placed on their points and separated by a blue print sash.

There seems to be no dedication block indicating for whom this quilt was made. But the names belong predominantly to members of the Middletown (Bucks County, Pennsylvania) Hicksite Quaker Meeting, who lived in the surrounding communities of Green Plain, Soulbury, Fallsington, Newtown and Upper Makefield. The dates found on some of the blocks range from 1845 to 1849.

Although the blocks are larger and the patterns more varied than in the Worrall friendship quilt, the fabric choice is still

corner blocks, which are carefully executed in an *Oak Leaf* and *The Reel* variation (page 30). Surrounding the forty-nine blocks is a larger-scale cotton print. The interlining is cotton batting and the back is a cotton print, all quilted together with even, fine stitches. From the consistency in workmanship and continuity of fabrics and pattern, it seems likely that this quilt was executed by one or several talented needleworkers, and not by all those whose names appear on the blocks. □

restricted to small prints (some with glazed surfaces) that are precisely and finely pieced. As with the Worrall quilt, the printed cotton back and cotton interlining are anchored to the top with small, even quilting stitches. The needlework on both of these pieces is of the finest quality.

These quilts, with their wide variety of printed fabrics, may reflect the more liberal religious beliefs of their makers. As noted, both of these quilts bear the names of Hicksite Quaker members. The history of Quakerism in America, like that of most minority religious sects, is punctuated with numerous dissensions and splintering of groups within the general religious body. The major Quaker schism occurred in 1827, when a group of more liberal Friends, among them Elias Hicks, after whom the Hicksite movement was named, established separate Meetings.

These Hicksites actually accounted for about seventy per cent of the Philadelphia Yearly Meeting Quakers and were predominantly country people. Many were located in Maryland and New York, and some in Ohio. Orthodox Quakers consisted mainly of the highly sophisticated Philadelphia Quakers, as well as those in New England, North Carolina and Ohio, who gathered support from the English Friends.[26] After 1827, many communities had two separate Friends Meetings. Although there were bitter dissensions between these two groups, they were more alike than different in dealing with problems of the period, such as

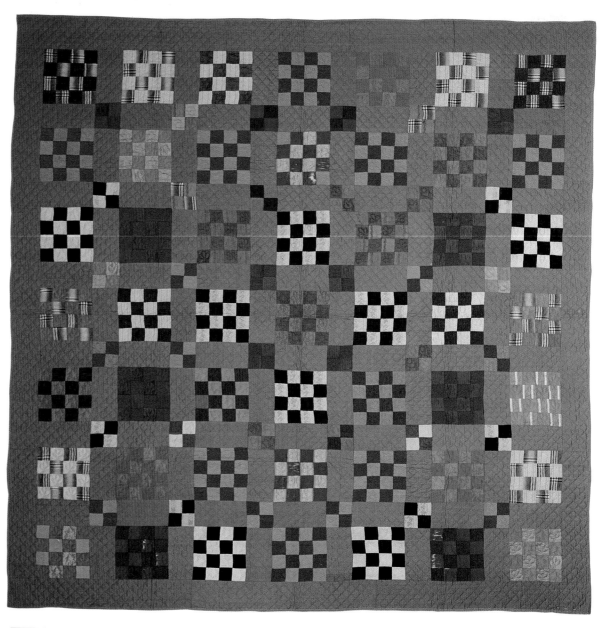

Sixteen *and* Four Patch, *attributed to Sarah W. Sharp Wills (1821–1879), Burlington County, New Jersey, 87 × 87 inches, pieced silks. Collection of Mrs. S. Kendrick Eshleman III.* □

Postcard view of the Cropwell Preparative Meeting near Marlton, New Jersey, taken in the early twentieth century. Collection of Mrs. S. Kendrick Eshleman III. □

temperance, slavery and education. Despite their disagreements, both were regarded by their contemporaries as Quakers. □

At the beginning of the second half of the nineteenth century, a wider range of silk fabrics appears to have been used in Quaker quilts. Two quilts belonging to Quaker families in Burlington County, New Jersey illustrate this point. While these more closely resemble patterns found in bedcoverings of the non-Quaker world than their silk predecessors, they still retain some of the color restraint so typical of the Friends' work.

The full-size *Sixteen* and *Four Patch* quilt (page 32), passed down in the Wills family of Burlington County, has as its background fabric a brownish silk. Its unusual hue has a quieting, harmonizing effect on the variety of other colored silk patches used. Although many of the silks are the browns, black, soft pinks and greens found in Quaker clothing of the period, brighter reds and blues have been introduced. These silks comprise not only plain-woven fabrics but also brocades and stripes. The silk top has been joined to the cotton interlining and robin's-egg-blue glazed cotton back by fine, even quilting stitches, in an overall diamond pattern. Within each colored silk square is quilted a small naturalistic leaf or floral motif. The edge is finished with a narrow pale brown silk binding.

Family history suggests that this quilt was made by the present owner's great-grand-mother, Sarah W. Sharp Wills, who was born in Burlington County in 1821 and died there in 1879. During her lifetime, Sarah was a member of the Cropwell Preparative Meeting (this page) near Marlton, New Jersey.

The other quilt (page 34), from this same meeting of New Jersey Friends, is a doll quilt that belonged to the Cooper family. It is thought to have been made by Lydia Evans Cooper, wife of Benjamin Cooper (1834–1876), for the children of the family. The current owner has fond childhood memories of this piece being used as a doll's covering. The top of this small quilt is pieced from striped silks alternating with plain-colored silk triangles. The edging is brown silk, and the back is a plain-woven glazed white cotton. Again, this piece displays visual restraint, with the interspersing of brown and tans among the brighter red, blue and green striped materials.[27]

The owner of this little piece recalls visiting her Quaker grandparents in New Jersey in the 1930's and 1940's. At that time, the women were still wearing long, dark, rustling silk dresses and matching bonnets, while the men held to their plain dark Quaker-style suits. She remembers that her grandparents also retained Quaker speech patterns, addressing people as "thee" and "thou." It is probable that the old traditions were slower to die out in the rural areas of Burlington County, New Jersey and Chester

BRIAN R. TOLBERT

Doll quilt sewn of triangles, attributed to Lydia Evans Cooper, Burlington County, New Jersey, c. 1860, 15¾ × 18½ inches, pieced silks. Collection of Mrs. S. Kendrick Eshleman III. □

Quaker quilts, like their makers, reflect various levels of social standing and religious liberalism. As with other religious sects, moderation in dress and style is reflected in the quilted bedcoverings of the Quakers. Expensive, though subtle, silks prevail in Quaker quilts well into the twentieth century. And although the Quakers employed printed and textured fabrics in their quilts, these works lack the exuberance found in other American quilts of the period. Quaker quilts are testimonies to their pasts; they seem to mirror the overall commitment their makers made to their beliefs. These principles were aptly summed up by the prominent American Quaker Isaac Norris I, in a letter written in 1707 or 1708: "Thus then, every man ought soberly and discreetly to set bounds to himself, and avoid extremes, still bearing due regard to the society he is of." [28] □

Outside of Pennsylvania and New Jersey, which are mentioned prominently in this article, notable seventeenth-century Quaker settlements were located in Rhode Island, New York, Virginia and North Carolina. Surely many unrecorded Quaker quilts are still owned by descendants of these early families. It is important to document and photograph these bedcoverings before those who retain the oral histories pass on. Although some scholarly work has been done about Quaker furniture and needlework, their quilts have been, with few exceptions, ignored. It is to be hoped that Patricia Herr's remarkable research will lead other quilt enthusiasts to add to her valuable documentation of Quaker quilts.

—Michael Kile

County, Pennsylvania than in the larger cities of Philadelphia, Trenton and Baltimore.

Quakers continued their quilting tradition through the late nineteenth and into the twentieth century, as is illustrated by a 1906 photograph of Quaker women quilting (page 23). The quilts of this period gradually assumed attributes of non-Quaker bedcoverings. There remained a predominance of block-style quilts, largely of silk with a more varied color palette. Repetitive designs and color restraint uncommon in their Victorian counterparts prevailed, yet *Crazy* quilts were made in large numbers by the Quakers. □

REFERENCE LIST

1. George Fox, *Journal*, (London, 1694), p. 317, as quoted in Allen C. Thomas and Richard H. Thomas, *A History of the Friends in America* (Philadelphia: The John C. Winston Co., 1905), p. 42.

2. J. William Frost, "Years of Crisis and Separation: Philadelphia Yearly Meeting, 1790-1860," Chapter II of *Friends in the Delaware Valley: Philadelphia Yearly Meeting 1681-1981*, edited by John M. Moore (Haverford, Pennsylvania: Friends Historical Association, 1981), p. 15.

3. J. William Frost, *The Quaker Family in Colonial America* (New York: St. Martin's Press, 1973), p. 177.

4. Robert C. Moon, M.D., *The Morris Family of Philadelphia, Descendants of Anthony Morris* (Philadelphia: Robert C. Moon, M.D., 1898), pp. 549-551.

5. Beatrice Garvan, unpublished research. Receipt books for these expenditures are still in the possession of a descendant and of the Historical Society of Pennsylvania, Philadelphia.

6. *Extracts from the Journal of Elizabeth Drinker*, edited by Henry Biddle (Philadelphia, 1889), n. pag.

7. Linda Parry and Natalie Rothstein, Victoria and Albert Museum, London, letter of April 12, 1984 to the author.

8. Averil Colby, *Quilting* (New York: Charles Scribner's Sons, 1971), frontispiece.

9. *Ibid.*, p. 26.

10. Leanna Lee-Whitman, "The Silk Trade: Chinese Silks and the British East India Company," *Winterthur Portfolio*, 17, No. 1 (1982), 28.

11. Beatrice Garvan, unpublished research, Coates Account Book, Pennsylvania Historical Society, Philadelphia.

12. Phrase used by Quaker John Reynall in 1738, when he wrote to David Flennegin in London to order furniture, including "2 raised Japan'd Black Corner Cubbards, with 2 Doors to each, no Red in 'em, of the best Sort, but Plain." Quoted in Frederick

B. Tolles, *Meeting House and Counting House: The Quaker Merchants of Colonial Philadelphia 1682-1763* (New York: W. W. Norton & Company, Inc., 1963), p. 128.

13. *Ibid.*, pp. 126-127.

14. *Ibid.*, p. 127.

15. Peter Kalm, *Peter Kalm's Travels in North America: The America of 1750*, trans. Adolf Benson (New York, 1937), II, 651.

16. Tolles, p. 8.

17. *The Works of George Fox* (Philadelphia, 1831), as quoted in Frost, *The Quaker Family*, p. 194.

18. Tolles, p. 125.

19. *Ibid.*, p. 239.

20. Frost, *The Quaker Family*, p. 188.

21. *Ibid.*, p. 187.

22. Two other Quaker silk quilts of this period are illustrated in publications by Susan Burrows Swan: *A Winterthur Guide to American Needlework* (New York: Crown Publishers, Inc., 1976), p. 111, fig. 80; *Plain and Fancy: American Women and Their Needlework, 1700-1850* (New York: Rutledge Books, 1977), p. 203, fig. 113.

23. Colby, pp. 115, 116, 132.

24. *Ibid.*, p. 22.

25. *Drinker*, Nov. 20, 1758; Jan. 15, 1759; June 23, 1760.

26. Frost, "Years of Crisis," p. 57.

27. Other Quaker pieced silk quilts that relate to these later bedcoverings are photographed and described in Shiela Betterton, *Quilts and Coverlets from the American Museum in Britain* (Frome and London: Butler and Tanner Ltd, 1978), pp. 30, 49, 50.

28. Tolles, p. 124. □

Special recognition is due Paul Flack, whose pioneer interest and enthusiasm for his own fine collection of Quaker quilts led to this undertaking.

Silhouette, attributed to August Edouart, done in Philadelphia on January 28, 1843, of Miss Julianna Jenks, seated with her sewing. Although painting was officially forbidden, Friends had no testimony against creating a cutout profile with scissors and dark paper. Silhouette cut by Helen and Ned Laughon from an original portfolio of duplicates, owned by the Friends Historical Library, Swarthmore College, Swarthmore, Pennsylvania. □

PATRICIA T. HERR is a veterinarian who lives and practices in Lancaster, Pennsylvania. With her husband, Donald M. Herr, she collects Southeastern Pennsylvania antiques of the eighteenth and nineteenth centuries. Her collecting interests include quilts, other needlework and hand-woven textiles of this Pennsylvania German area. She has written and lectured about Pennsylvania German textiles, and has served as curator for several exhibitions. She was a guest curator for "The Pennsylvania Germans: A Celebration of Their Arts, 1683-1850," an exhibition organized by the Philadelphia Museum of Art and The Henry Francis du Pont Winterthur Museum, Inc. of Delaware.

THE AUTHOR wishes to thank the following people who have not already been mentioned and who, in many ways, helped make this article possible: Susan Anderson, Curator of Textiles, and Conna Clark, Rights and Reproductions, Philadelphia Museum of Art; Richard B. Chalfont; Ruth Hagy, Curator of Collections, and Rosmary B. Philips, Librarian, Chester County Historical Society, West Chester, Pennsylvania; Elizabeth Meg Shaefer, assistant curator, Louise Steinman Von Hess Foundation, Lancaster County, Pennsylvania; and the staff of the Friends Historical Library, Swarthmore College, Swarthmore, Pennsylvania.

SHOWCASE

COMPILED BY RODERICK KIRACOFE

Memory Jars, by Terrie Hancock Mangat, Cincinnati, Ohio, 1984, 48 × 31 inches, appliquéd and pieced cotton blends and novelty fabrics, tied. Techniques include reverse appliqué and embroidery. Embellished with personal mementos. Titled, signed and dated in embroidery. This quilt was inspired by a memory jar belonging to the quiltmaker's grandmother. Collection of the quiltmaker.

Feathered Star, 1880–1900, Ohio, 91 ½ × 89 inches, pieced cottons with embroidery. Collection of American Horse Antiques and Folk Art, Southfield, Michigan.

Princess Feather and *Rose of Sharon,* by Lutheria Babbitt Johnson, Bomoseen, Vermont, c. 1860, 85 × 79½ inches, appliquéd cottons. Private collection. Submitted by the Vermont Quilt Festival, Northfield, Vermont.

39

Political, c. 1880–1900, found in Pennsylvania, 86 × 85 inches, pieced cottons. At the center is a commemorative handkerchief with pictures of James A. Garfield and Chester A. Arthur, Republican Presidential and Vice-Presidential candidates in the election of 1880. Collection of Shelly Zegart's Quilts, Louisville, Kentucky.

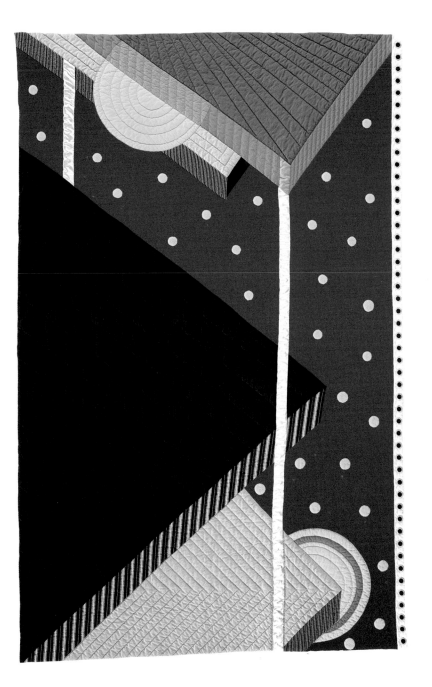

Sunflower, by Cherry
Partee, Seattle, 1984,
47 × 74 inches, appliquéd
cottons, cotton blends
and lamé. Collection of
Gail Kirgis. Courtesy of
The Hissing Goose,
Ketchum, Idaho.

Unknown pattern,
c. 1930–1940, Ohio
Amish, 69 × 73 inches,
pieced cottons.
Collection of Dale
Duesing.

*F*oggy Interweave, by
Miriam Nathan-Roberts,
Berkeley, California,
1984, 57 × 56 inches,
machine-pieced cottons.
Hand-quilted by Sarah
Hershberger, Charm,
Ohio. This quilt is one of
a series. Collection of
Miriam Nathan-Roberts.

Variable Star,
c. 1830–1850, Pennsyl-
vania, 92 × 77 inches,
pieced cottons.
Collection of Dr. and
Mrs. James Lodge,
Irvine, California. (See
cover for a detail of this
quilt.)

Self-Portrait, by Kristin Marx Meuser, San Francisco, 1974, 36 × 28 inches, appliquéd canvas, cotton blends, wool and synthetics, quilted by machine. Techniques include needlepoint and padding. This work is based on a photograph of the maker at age four. Collection of Joanne and Robert Meuser.

Shooting Gallery, by
Linda MacDonald,
Willits, California, 1983,
82 × 92 inches,
machine-pieced and
hand-appliquéd cottons,
some of which are
hand-dyed. Quilted by
hand. Collection of the
quiltmaker.

Migration, by Judy Mathieson, Woodland Hills, California, 1984, 70 × 88 inches, hand-appliquéd and machine-pieced cottons. Quilted by hand. The Dutch wax prints which form the background scene have been pieced to the fabrics which form the lattice. Additional motifs have been appliquéd to some of these patches. Collection of the quiltmaker.

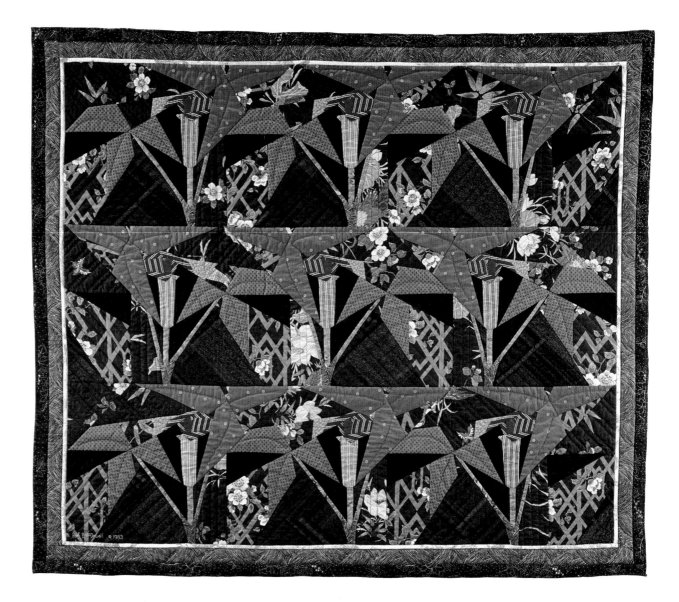

Jack-in-the-Pulpit,
© 1983 Ruth B.
McDowell, Winchester,
Massachusetts, 60 ½ × 51
inches, machine-pieced
and hand-quilted cottons
and cotton blends. Signed
and dated in embroidery.
Collection of George and
Marilyn Pobedinsky.

Basket of Flowers,
c. 1860–1880,
Pennsylvania, 87 × 80
inches, appliquéd
cottons. Techniques
include piping along the
inside edge of the
binding, as well as
padding. Collection of
Joseph M. B. Sarah,
Cambridge City, Indiana.

49

Outlooks, by Barbara L. Crane, Lexington, Massachusetts, 1984, 58 × 52 inches, pieced by hand and machine, and hand-quilted in cottons and cotton blends, some hand-dyed. Each view is embellished with a different miniature object. Collection of the quiltmaker.

Telestar, © 1984 Joan
Schulze, Sunnyvale,
California, 48 ½ × 42 ½
inches, appliquéd and
pieced hand-dyed and
painted cottons and silks,
with Xerox transfer.
Signed and dated in
embroidery. Collection of
the quiltmaker.

51

Common Ground, by Rhoda Cohen, Weston, Massachusetts, 1983–1984, 66½ × 104 inches, pieced by hand and machine, and hand-appliquéd in wools and wool blends. Quilted by hand. Techniques include embroidery, reverse appliqué and tying. Titled, signed and dated in embroidery. Collection of the quiltmaker.

Washington Island, by
Edward Larson,
Libertyville, Illinois, and
Cathy Grafton, Pontiac,
Illinois, 1983,
53½ × 68½ inches, hand-
appliquéd and pieced by
hand and machine in
cottons, many of which
are tea-dyed, with
embroidery. Quilted by
hand. Signed and dated
in embroidery. Collection
of the quiltmakers.
Courtesy of Monique
Knowlton Gallery,
Chicago.

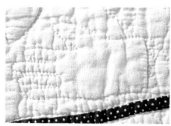

Unknown pattern,
c. 1860–1880, found in
Indiana, 82 × 63½
inches, pieced and
appliquéd cottons.
Quilted along one
outside border are hands
and sets of initials.
Collection of Shelly
Zegart's Quilts,
Louisville, Kentucky.

Shiraz, by Judy P. Cloninger, Seabrook, Texas, 1983, 68½ × 96 inches, pieced cottons. There are approximately five thousand pieces of fabric in this quilt. Collection of the quiltmaker.

Rose and Compass,
© 1984 Becky Kerns,
Grosse Ile, Michigan,
87 × 87 inches, appliquéd
and pieced cottons.
Techniques include
stuffed work, padding
and stipple quilting.
Signed and dated in
embroidery. Collection of
the quiltmaker.

Central Medallion, c. 1825–1835, American or English, 99 × 89½ inches, pieced and appliquéd cottons and cotton chintzes, cut for a poster bed. According to Florence M. Montgomery in *Printed Textiles,* the metal roller used to print the blue and white star-cluster print (third border from outside) was manufactured and sold to a Cheshire, England printworks in 1824. The chintzes are English. A white Marseille spread serves as the interlining. Collection of the Indianapolis Museum of Art (Miscellaneous Funds).

Album, made by members of the Oneida Community, Oneida, New York, 1873–1874, 89 × 84 inches, appliquéd cottons. Techniques include embroidery and ink work. This quilt was made for the wife of John Humphrey Noyes, founder of the Community. Women and men in the Community made enough blocks for two quilts, and the best were chosen for this one. (A second quilt was made with the leftover blocks.) Several blocks in this quilt depict the various activities of Community life. Collection of the Oneida Community Historical Committee, on permanent display at the Mansion House in Oneida, New York. Submitted by the American Textile Registry, Cazenovia, New York.

*S*olid Geometry, © 1984
Faye Anderson, Denver,
Colorado, 50 × 58 inches,
appliquéd cottons.
Collection of Mountain
Bell, Denver.

LONG REMEMBERED

AN ALABAMA PIONEER & HER QUILTS

The people who inherited from him came from the north-east, through the Tennessee mountains by stages marked by the bearing and raising of a generation of children. They came from the Atlantic seaboard and before that, from England and the Scottish and Welsh Marches.... They brought no slaves and no Phyfe and Chippendale highboys; indeed, what they did bring most of them could (and did) carry in their hands. They took up land and built one- and two-room cabins and never painted them, and married one another and produced children and added other rooms one by one to the original cabins and did not paint them either, but that was all. Their descendants still planted cotton in the bottom land and corn along the edge of the hills and in the

secret coves in the hills made whiskey of the corn and sold what they did not drink."

With some important changes, this passage from the opening pages of Faulkner's *The Hamlet* could describe my ancestors. In the nineteenth century, my great-grandfather's family came from the Carolinas into Georgia, then into Alabama, settling first in Blount County. Some, including my grandfather and his two brothers, would eventually move into adjacent Cullman County, and there they would remain. A few more daring individuals would relocate in Florida, and a handful of venturesome souls, cousins of my grandfather, were to push even farther west into unhospitable Texas territory.

They came not on foot, but in wagons with their few possessions; they were not sharecroppers, but the proud and industrious owners of small farms. They grew cotton, corn and enough tobacco for home use. They were hardworking, law-abiding, honest, independent, God-fearing fundamentalists and Democrats. I never heard of any illicit involvement with distilling. They certainly owned no slaves or Chippendale highboys. They were rather an intermediary farmer class, between Faulkner's Varners and Snopeses, belonging to that vast group out of which would rise a generation or so later the agrarian middle class of the South. [2]

The genteel tradition of plantation life that has come to be associated stereotypically with the ante-bellum South — the columned mansions, vast holdings of land, slaves, magnolias and mint juleps — never existed in the area settled by my great-grandfather's family, the hill country of northern Alabama. It is true that this elegant and refined lifestyle was known to some limited extent farther north in the fertile Tennessee Valley area, in that narrow band on either side of the Tennessee River stretching from Huntsville in the east to Florence in the west, but it was a more conspicuous part of life in what is known as the Alabama Black Belt,

BY ROBERT T. CARGO

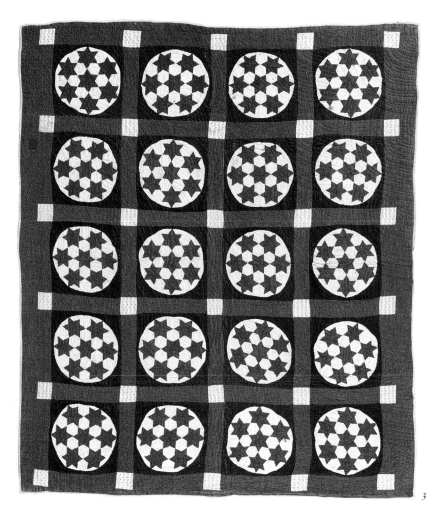

3

these two major geographical districts of the state. Go south and west from Tuscaloosa and you enter directly into the flat area that produced cotton, the cornerstone of the economy until World War II. Now those fields are converted into rich grazing land for herds of beef cattle. Go north from Tuscaloosa and you are abruptly in the hill country. The contrast is apt to shock the uninitiated.

My great-grandfather on the paternal side of my mother's family was William Mabrey Thomas, and his wife, Mary Ann, my great-grandmother (no. 2), had been a Rouse prior to their marriage on December 30, 1859. The Thomas family had moved into a remote corner of Blount County well before the Civil War, and it was from there that my great-grandparents' family emerged. There were thirteen children, six sons and seven daughters. I never knew either of these great-grandparents, for they both died before I was born.

Great-grandfather Mabrey Thomas was a foot soldier in the Confederate Army, serving as a private with Company F of the Twenty-ninth Alabama Infantry Regiment. During his absence, my great-grandmother was responsible for caring for the two small children who had been born by the time of her husband's induction into the military. She cultivated the crops herself, and money for the few necessities—coffee, flour and sugar—was obtained by selling vegetables in nearby Warrior and, on rare occasions, in Birmingham. My grandfather recalled in his old age that she had to do all this herself, in a cart, a wagon, a buggy, sometimes on horseback, or at times even on foot. Her courage and strength were an accepted part of family history, and one example was especially favored by my grandfather. Having left eleven-month-old son Bud under a tree beside the field where she was working, she returned to find a snake—a copperhead, my grandfather never failed to add—coiled up beside the sleeping child. My great-grandmother managed to separate the two, kill the snake and rescue the baby unharmed. Her courage was not sufficient, however, to save the family horse, taken off by a gang of Union soldiers in spite of her protests and in spite of its being hidden, along with

named for the rich, black, level land. A small, cultured class of Southern aristocracy lived in small but active centers having an agriculture-based economy, in towns like Eufaula, Montgomery, Prattville, Lowndesboro, Camden, Greensboro, Demopolis and Eutaw, where today descendants of that nineteenth-century lei-sured class struggle to preserve some vestige of the glory that once was. Tuscaloosa lies precisely on the line of demarcation separating other belongings, under the bluffs that lined the Warrior River near which stood their house.

Great-grandfather Mabrey Thomas lives, in my reveries at least, in part because of the Seth Thomas clock which marks the hours for my family today as it once did for his. That steeple-front clock standing on the shelf in my kitchen is the only object that has come down to me from him. If my knowledge of my great-grandfather is vague and distant, it is not the same, or so it seems, with Great-grandmother Mary Ann Rouse Thomas. Because of a number of her quilts that were passed on to me, and because of research into the family history inspired by those pieces, I feel a strong emotional bond with this woman I never knew. In the late 1950's, after I was married, my grandfather and grandmother, as a Christmas present one year, gave me a quilt. It was, he said, one that his mother had made. I was to learn later that the pattern was called *Seven Sisters* (no. 3). Ultimately, I acquired more of my great-grandmother's quilts—some that I received after my grandfather's death in 1971, some that were given to me by various family members—so that I now have nine of the quilts that she made. Two additional quilts have been located; they remain in the hands of two of the maker's granddaughters who have generously shared them, as now, whenever asked.

At some point after the gift of that first quilt, my grandfather passed on to me some old photographs. One of them (no. 1) showed a group of family members gathered in front of the Thomas home. By some stroke of good fortune, a concession perhaps to the anonymous, itinerant photographer's innate aesthetic

sense, four quilts had been hung on the porch, in all probability to enliven the drab, unpainted house that served as a background for the Blount County pioneer family portrait. Those quilts were made by my great-grandmother, who appears in the photograph wearing the dark dress with the white apron. My grandfather, James William, through whose hands most of the quilts came to me, is shown with the banjo. Other family members (their relationships indicated with respect to my grandfather) include, front row, left to right: William Mabrey Thomas (1836–1900), bearded, with gun, father; Luceina Caroline Thomas Robbins (1872–1962), sister; Beatrice Robbins Foster (1895–1979), Luceina's daughter; Della Thomas (1887–1972), sister; Walter Thomas (1880–1972), brother; Jeff Thomas (1888–1980), the youngest brother; Mary Ann Rouse Thomas (1842–1930), in apron, mother; James William Thomas (1878–1971), with banjo, my grandfather; Charlie McAnnally, a family friend; Thomas Robbins, on horseback, Luceina's husband, holding their daughter, Mary Ann. Back row, left to right: Dee Thomas, a first cousin; John Henry Thomas (1876–1973), brother; and Bud Thomas (1862–1949), with gun, the oldest brother. The photograph is most reliably dated by the age of the child who is held by her father, the man on horseback. That child, Mary Ann Robbins, was born on January 28, 1897. It seems, therefore, that 1899 is the most logical date to assign to the picture, for this must be a two-year-old child, her third winter as it were, for the small, leafless tree in the center indicates the dormant season.

The photograph offers an intimate glimpse into the unadorned and simple life of a pioneer family in remote Alabama at the very end of the nineteenth century, as well as being a remarkable, if not unique, piece of documentation of nineteenth-century quilts and persons. Whereas we generally must depend upon oral history for the documentation of old quilts, I know of no other early photograph that serves not

only to date now-existing works but serves also as documentary evidence of their maker and their place of origin. Almost miraculously, of that group, three quilts have been preserved and remain in the family.

Of my great-grandmother's quilts in the photograph, the first (left to right) appears to be a version of *Tree of Life* and it is the one of the four that has been lost. No family member has any recollection of the quilt, and it has apparently vanished without so much as a trace except for this picture. This is not surprising when one remembers that until only quite recently most quilts were considered to be mere household goods, held with indifference if not contempt, items that could always be replaced. Evaluating quilts as folk art is an idea that, with few exceptions, has arisen in only the last fifteen years.

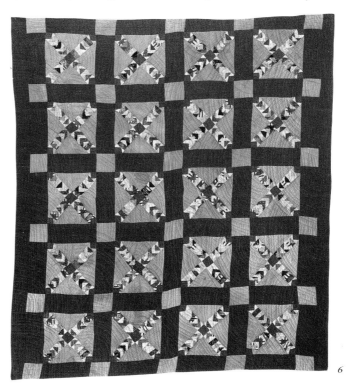

The second quilt, the *Snail Trail* (no. 4) as it is known in the family, belongs to a cousin and granddaughter of the maker, Lillian Thomas Seibert, whose father, John Henry, appears on the porch in the photograph. *Snail Trail* is a pattern that I have encountered only here in Alabama, and then only to a limited degree. Perhaps it will be recognized by readers in other parts of the country, but I know of no quilt books that show the pattern by this or any other name. Because of the slight curvature required for all its pieces, it is not an easy pattern to handle, and this may account in part for its rarity. This quilt served as the background for a photograph of my grandfather (no. 5) taken inside the house on the same day as the group photograph.

6

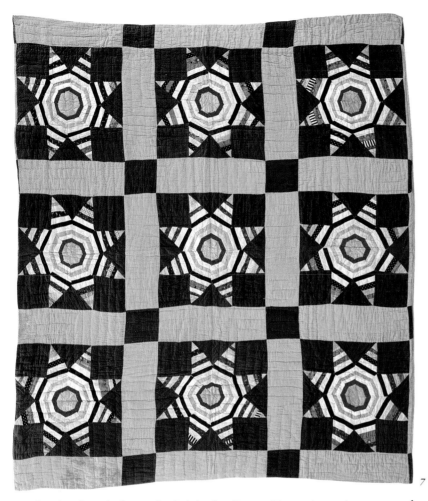

7

The third quilt from the left is the *Seven Sisters* (no. 3), so named for the constellation Pleiades, the first of my great-grandmother's quilts that I received. I suspect that she was thinking of her own seven daughters when at work on this quilt. Like *Snail Trail*, this is a difficult pattern to work; six-pointed stars are less frequently seen than eight-pointed ones, which are easier to handle since they are based on the quadrant.

The quilt hanging on the extreme right is a *Wild Goose Chase* (no. 6), one with exceedingly large corner blocks, a quilt that belonged to my uncle, Willie Benson Thomas (1903–1975). It was

added to the collection as a gift from his widow, my aunt, Vera Jones Thomas.

Superior is a second *Wild Goose Chase* (no. 8). Due to adept color arrangement, the visual effect produced is that of the *Variable Star* pattern scattered over the surface of the quilt, and the eye is drawn to these sparkling blue stars that stand at the center of the blocks. This *Wild Goose Chase* is a fine example of Mary Ann Rouse Thomas's well-developed, though intuitive, sense of color and design.

Aesthetically speaking, however, a surviving *Tree of Life* (no. 9) represents what most would probably agree to be the apex of the quiltmaking art of my great-grandmother. The quilt, to my mind, must be considered as one of the truly great examples of Southern folk art. It is a quilt that can hold its own against the very best pieces of this type. The capricious handling of the black stripping around the outer edges of the four trees set in the corners of the quilt is especially interesting. Un-like the conventional technique, my great-grandmother stopped the black before each corner, at the points where the diamond touches the outer edge. She then placed one black strip bisecting the angle of the outer corner. There is a naïve, child-like quality in these black lines that seem almost to be drawn in ink, and rather crudely. The effect is dramatic and startling, and caused one highly respected quilt and folk-art dealer who recently saw the quilt to comment, "Your great-grandmother must have been a liberated woman." I confess that I had never thought of her in those terms, but I knew

8

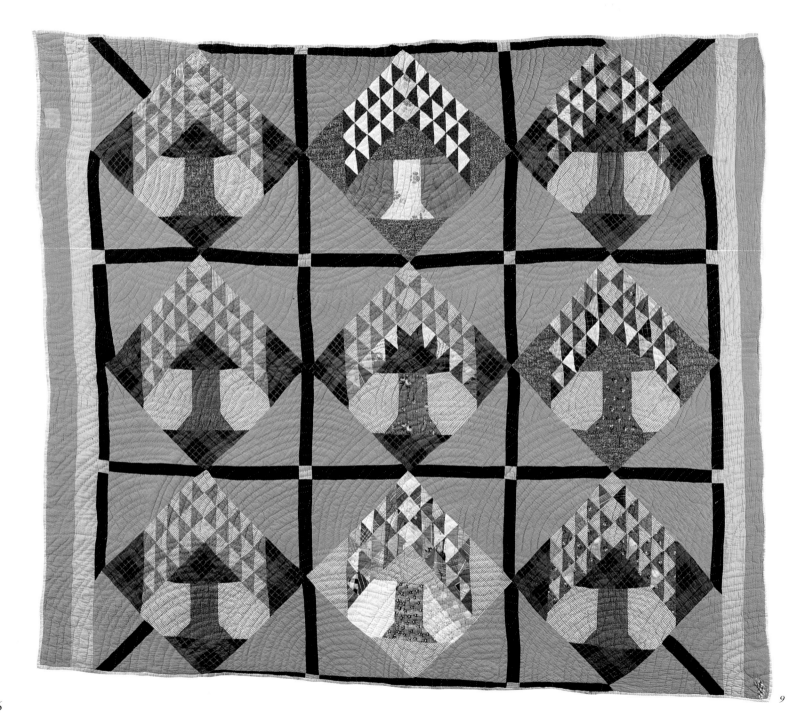

what was meant, for she was, by all accounts, a woman of great strength and independence, and the quilt radiates those qualities.

Each of the latter two quilts, the *Tree of Life* and the *Wild Goose Chase* with blue, has a small scrap of brown-and-white checked cloth (no. 10) sewn in one corner. These scraps served as identification tags for those times when the quilts were lent, perhaps to neighbors or relatives, for use when an influx of company required extra quilts for cover or for pallets made on the floor. Visits frequently necessitated overnight stays; deaths, likewise, brought extended visits from kinfolk. At such times, neighbors were expected to join the bereaved family and sit up around the corpse, which was laid out in the coffin. On these occasions, people sat and slept in alternating periods of three to four hours.

The boldly executed *Spider-web Star* (no. 7), set on blue blocks, was given to me by my aunt, Ola Thomas Caldwell. Rather than the cotton filling that is found in all the other quilts made by my great-grandmother, the filler used in this piece is an old quilt. Such practice was common in an age when nothing was discarded; worn-out quilts and blankets were frequently put to such use. These practices can usually be detected because of an unusual stiffness that results. The backing of this quilt is composed of pieces of coarsely-woven cloth, sacks mainly, home-dyed in a brown probably obtained from walnut hulls. The persistent lettering of one sack from the Henderson Sugar Refinery in New Orleans proclaims, "Flavor With Sugar and You Flavor With Health." Two other quilts, the *Tree of Life* (no. 9) and a *Carpenter's Wheel* (no. 11),

11

have backings partially pieced of such bags, with varying commercial imprints.

The visual power of most of my great-grandmother's quilts derives to a substantial degree from the unusually wide sashing she employed between blocks. Her utilization of this technique is aptly demonstrated in *Le Moyne Star* (no. 12). She took a quite ordinary pattern and gave it a fresh interpretation.

One quilt of the group, the *Carpenter's Wheel* (no. 11), represents in its top the work of several women. It is a friendship quilt, and was the result of the co-operative efforts of some family members and some "old girl friends" my grandfather was fond of recalling. His mother was responsible for completing the requisite number of blocks, setting them together, and for the quilting. Five blocks carry signatures, one of which was that of Lizzie Thomas, the sister of Mabrey, that is, my grandfather's aunt.

A second friendship quilt was made for my grandfather's brother, John Henry. The two brothers were married five days apart in December of 1902. The quilts, therefore, probably date from around 1900, since it is safe to assume that both were made prior to the marriages: maiden ladies would have hardly involved themselves in work of such a personal nature for married men, personal especially in the case of John Henry's quilt with its declaration "I love you," albeit concealed in Latin. Neither quilt, by the way, has the signature of the women who, a few years hence, were to become the brides of these two swains. This second quilt is in a pattern known as *Pontiac Star* (no. 13). A few squares bear the name or initials of the donors. As with the first quilt, my great-grandmother was responsible for completing the required blocks, assembling them and doing the quilting.

The star in various forms and arrangements is the most frequently encountered pattern in her quilts. Of the seven star quilts, five are based on the eight-pointed shape made of diamond-cut pieces. That is the case with *Blazing Star* (no. 14), which most likely represents a co-operative effort on the part of my great-grandmother and my grandmother, the top having been made by the former and the quilting done by the latter.

12

The last quilt made by my great-grandmother that we have knowledge of is a *Variable Star* (no. 15). It was made as a gift in 1928 for the fifth birthday of a cousin, the maker's granddaughter, Belva Thomas Cheatham, whose father, Walter, is shown in the family photograph.

My great-grandmother's quilts are typical of those made in northern Alabama until recent years. They are generally small quilts, and most are composed *13* of sets of twenty or thirty repeating blocks. They were intended to cover the top of the bed only, with perhaps a bit hanging over the sides, and were never planned as coverlets such as those we associate with the plantation tradition in the South. Regularly in this type of quilt, the bindings are formed by trimming the backing material to the appropriate width and bringing it over the top. The quilting tends to be coarse and must

be considered functional rather than decorative. My great-grandmother's quilting was most often done, or so it seems in the quilts we have here for evidence, in what the family calls "shells." The first quilting arc was marked with a soft-leaded pencil or a piece of chalk tied onto a string, the end of which was held down firmly while the free hand would swing the instrument around, marking the line to be quilted. The inner, smaller concentric arcs could then be quilted freehand, or they could be marked in the manner of the first arc.

Generally speaking, the strong design qualities apparent in this group of quilts and their delightful spontaneity obviously exceed their needlework. Untrained and working in isolation in the true folk-art tradition, Mary Ann Rouse Thomas proceeded with an intuitive knowledge of color and pattern.

For the nineteenth century, or any century for that matter, my great-grandmother lived an exceedingly long life, a family characteristic shared by nearly all of her thirteen children. One way perhaps to grasp the scope of this lifetime of eighty-eight years is to project it against the panorama of American history. Born in 1842, during the tenure of the tenth president of the United States, John Tyler, she lived through the terms of the next twenty-one presidents, to die during the Great Depression while Herbert Hoover was in office. She saw the great upheaval of the Civil War, the freeing of the slaves, the presidency of Abraham Lincoln and, in the early part of this century, a world war. Had she not smoked a pipe, she might have lived to be a hundred.

As is known, her life was affected directly by the Civil War—the hardships resulting from the

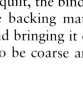

14

68

15

absence of a husband, gone to do battle for the Confederacy, a wife and mother left alone with the responsibilities of rearing two children during that difficult time. On one occasion, it is said that she traveled by horse all the way from her home to Huntsville—a distance of some seventy-five miles—to procure salt, a commodity virtually impossible to find in the South as the War Between the States wore on. Nor did the influence of this war end for my great-grandmother with the cessation of hostilities. Several years after the death of my great-grandfather, a fall left her with a broken hip. Poorly attended following this injury, she never walked again. Some years after the fall, in an application signed with her mark, an "X" (I think she never learned to write or perhaps to read either), she successfully petitioned the state for a pension as the widow of a Confederate soldier. Confined to a wheelchair for the rest of her days, she whiled away the hours making quilts (there must have been dozens) and yard after yard of knitted lace.

With no passing thought of recognition, with no vain dream of glory and with the indefatigable and stoic devotion of a Sisyphus, she kept diligently at her labors throughout her life. She would have been the last to imagine that she would be remembered long after her passing for a few quilts that survive her.

In *Remembrance of Things Past,* the French novelist Marcel Proust wrote about a Celtic belief that he subscribed to:

> I find that Celtic belief quite plausible—the idea that the souls of those we have lost are held captive in some lower form of life, an animal, a plant or an inanimate thing, lost to us in effect until that day, which for many never comes, when we happen to pass by that tree, or come into possession of that object which is their prison; then those souls begin to stir, they call out to us, and no sooner have we recognized them than the spell is broken. Liberated by us, they have overcome death and return to life with us.

I believe that we all share in this Celtic belief to some extent, to varying degrees, of course, and frequently only on a subconscious level, and for many of us, the past lives on in the present through the quilts of a bygone age. My great-grandmother's soul stirs within her quilts, and I, thankfully, have been witness to its recurrent awakenings.

ROBERT T. CARGO is Professor of Romance Languages at The University of Alabama, Tuscaloosa. With his wife, Helen, he has collected quilts for nearly thirty years. Started with his great-grandmother's quilts, today their collection numbers over four hundred examples, most of which are from Alabama.

FOR HER INITIAL and continuing interest in this group of quilts, the author wishes to thank Gail Andrews Trechsel, former Curator of Decorative Arts at the Birmingham Museum of Art, who sought out and recognized the significance of the collection.

OUT OF CONTROL

QUILTS THAT BREAK THE RULES

by Barbara Brackman

Traditional quiltmakers, like poets, express their creativity within definite and established forms. The rules for American quilts, which govern format, design and material, although inherent, are as specific and established as the more formally communicated rules for a sonnet or haiku.

These rules, such as those for format (the quilt shape and size), are rarely specified. By looking, quiltmakers learn, for example, that quilts have squared corners: they fit on beds. It is not until we see this format rule ignored that we realize how important is the unspoken law of the squared corner to our concept of a quilt.

The rules of design have been communicated over generations by both word and example. Design principles governing, for example, the repetition of the block are basic to the appearance of the American quilt, whether the design is a simple *Nine Patch* that we enjoy for its calm, repetitive rhythm or a more complex *Old Maid's Puzzle* that dares us to determine where one block ends and another begins. We have been trained to expect symmetry or repetitive patterns in a quilt design.

Rules also limit the fabric which goes into a quilt. For example, many quilts are composed of cotton calicoes, the small-scale prints that can easily be blended into appliqué and pieced designs. Plaids, stripes and cabbage roses are found less often, since strong prints can more easily overwhelm a delicately detailed pattern.

Conventions such as these give quilters a secure framework within which their ideas can flourish. Given the accepted constraints, myriad variations ensure quilting's continuing appeal to needleworkers. Those of us who never tire of looking at quilts and their patterns delight in the ways a right triangle can be used, in the pattern possibilities growing from a simple square and in the numerous applications of the *Log Cabin* block. Each new discovery adds to our understanding of a pattern, rather than boring us with its repetition. Even the ubiquitous *Grandmother's Flower Garden* offers us the pleasant satisfaction of examining each new circle of hexagons to find flowers carefully cut from scraps of fabric and placed into the wreath. We find joy in viewing each quiltmaker's personal exploration within the boundaries of the rules.

Nevertheless, it is also satisfying to come upon a quilt which breaks these rules. The quilt which flouts convention can be enjoyed on many levels. We can be charmed by its outrageous disregard of precedent; we can marvel at its striking, intuitive design qualities; we can admire the perseverance of the maker who completed the project despite design problems or limited craftsmanship.

Although some of the unusual quilts presented here display limited craftsmanship, they cannot be summarily dismissed as merely "bad quilts." The artistic instincts of the makers transcend the poverty of materials and sewing abilities. Uninhibited by traditions of either fine art or folk art, and possessing an intuitive creativity, these artists show us new ways to look at fabric, format and quilt design. For example, in the pink and yellow *Nine Patch* (no. 1), the maker's strong sense of color elevates the quilt above the average. Edward Faust (the maker of quilt number 5) and Theonia Caltas (the maker of quilt number 6) used fabric in ways

1. *Nine Patch* variation, c. 1930–1950, found in Kansas, 70½ × 81 inches, pieced cottons. Collection of the author.

Was this quilter ignorant of how quilts are supposed to look? Or was there an adventurous disregard for conservative concepts like squared corners? Why did the quilter adhere to principles of design repeat part of the time, and adapt or ignore them at other times? Did the quilter lose touch with reality at some point, or was there some unique and subtle intention at work? We can only wonder at the persistence of the unknown quiltmaker, who persevered, without thought to squared corners and design repeats, to the last of the enormous quilting stitches.

that have merits beyond mere naivety; they created with the fabrics of their eras in ways that few others attempted, and they succeeded.

Three of the artists represented here remain anonymous, and we can only speculate upon the circumstances which led them to disregard the conventions. But even the identities of a few makers and interviews with surviving relatives offer us inadequate answers to our questions about how and why these quilts came to look as they do. Fortunately, our visual enjoyment of a quilt rarely requires any knowledge of its source. However, any admirer of the unconventional quilt should be familiar with recent work by students of ethnic variations in quiltmaking. Exhibits organized by Maude Wahlman[1] and Roland Freeman,[2] for example, point out that the work of black quiltmakers living in isolated communities does not follow the rules of mainstream quiltmaking. It follows, instead, a community aesthetic developed from African roots. The quilts shown here share many characteristics with the Afro-American quilts—a disregard for design repeat, a jazz-like quality of theme and variations, a lack of concern for traditional concepts of craftsmanship; the result can be spontaneous and lively quilts. It is even possible, therefore, that some of the anonymous quilts here may be part of the Afro-American quilt tradition.

At the very least, it is obvious that each of these quiltmakers was guided by a personal vision to create a quilt that appeals to the eye, the imagination and the sense of whimsy.

REFERENCE LIST

1. Maude Wahlman, "The Art of Afro-American Quiltmaking: Origin, Development and Significance." Ph.D. dissertation, Yale University, 1980.

2. Roland Freeman, *Something to Keep You Warm: The Roland Freeman Collection of Black American Quilts from the Mississippi Heartland*, Exhibition catalogue (Jackson: Mississippi Department of Archives and History, 1981).

3. *Folk Art in Oklahoma.* Catalogue of an exhibition presented by the Oklahoma Museums Association, Oklahoma City, 1981.

BARBARA BRACKMAN is a writer specializing in quilts and other folk arts. She lives in Lawrence, Kansas. She is the author and publisher of *An Encyclopedia of Pieced Quilt Patterns*, an index to pattern names. Her work on quilt history appears regularly in *Quilter's Newsletter Magazine* and other publications.

2. *North Carolina Lily*, c. 1880–1910, origin unknown, 50 × 60 inches, pieced and appliquéd cottons. Collection of Merikay Waldvogel, Knoxville, Tennessee.

The anonymous maker of the North Carolina Lily *also rejected the conventional design repeat. The traditional nineteenth-century pattern is set symmetrically in the center of the quilt, but the bordering pattern disintegrates from the left to the right side. Its abstract, four-lobed flowers or leaves (an odd choice to border the dainty lilies) appear intact only in the left-hand row. They are made of the same fabric as the very precise lilies, and therefore were most likely made by the same person; if not, perhaps a second person finished the quilt. But with such seemingly total disregard for the structured central pattern? Or was there but one quilter, who from the very beginning intended to create a quilt which combines stark precision and convention with such radical individuality? There are many mysteries for us in this quilt, and the mysteries themselves are fascinating.*

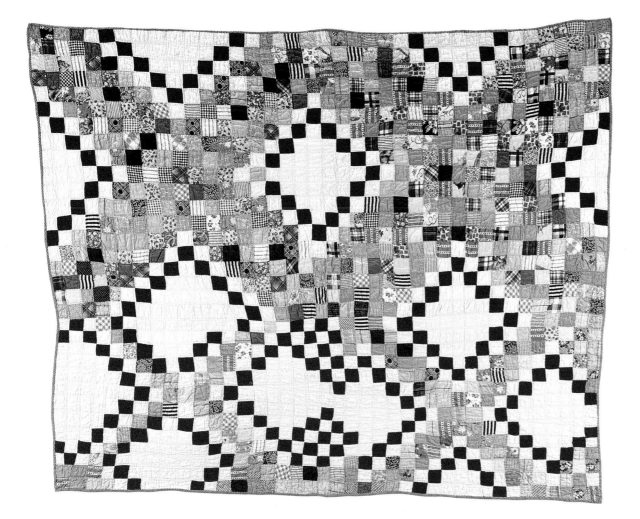

3. *Rainbow Round the World,* by Marcena Coffman McNabb, Oklahoma, c. 1935–1950, 76 × 60½ inches, pieced cottons and cotton blends. Collection of Larry Johnson.

The rhythm set up by the design repeat in Marcena Coffman McNabb's Rainbow Round the World *quilt is jarring. The very ordered pattern in the upper half is transformed in the lower half; there is a clash between the orderly and a distortion of it. It does appear that the quilt is out of the maker's control, but this is just one of the many unusual quilts she made during the later years of her life. Marcena's family recalls that she made conventional quilts for most of her life, but then her patchwork lost its restraint. Most of the later work was left as unquilted tops, but Mary Ann Anders and Chris Salmon, who were charmed by the expressive visual qualities in Marcena's work, had some of the tops quilted and they displayed them in a 1980 exhibition,* Folk Art in Oklahoma.[3]

4. *Hexagon,* by Marcena Coffman McNabb, Oklahoma, c. 1935–1950, 95 × 75 inches, pieced cottons and cotton blends, quilted later. Collection of Mary Ann Anders, Oklahoma City, Oklahoma.

Like so many folk artists who do their most creative work in their retirement years, Marcena Coffman McNabb seems to have been freed from a concern for what others might think. She made many variations of the Hexagon *pattern, each unique in its approach to the use of fabric, design repeat and format. In this example we see a sure ability to cut and piece precisely, but the quilt itself is unconventional and unrestrained. The patterns which are formed by the carefully crafted hexagons are several and disjointed; the pieces of the body and of the border are careful and regular, but the quilt appears as though it happened by accident, as if Marcena was guided by her needle, not conversely.*

5. Central Medallion, by Edward McKeen Faust, Berryton, Kansas, c. 1915–1935, 59 × 66½ inches, pieced cottons. Edward Faust's wife died in 1903, leaving him with three sons, aged three, five and six years. Edward raised his sons, doing all the cooking, canning, cleaning, laundering and sewing. This quilt belongs to a grandson, Ira J. Faust of Overbrook, Kansas, son of Ira D. Faust, who was six years old at the time of his mother's death.

The mention of pieced quilts generally calls to mind delicate calico prints joined into complex geometric designs. It is an unwritten rule that the print of the fabric should not interfere with the quilt pattern. Edward Faust overlooked the traditional dominance of piecing over print. Possessing a wonderfully intuitive sense of design, Edward created a flamboyant Central Medallion quilt with a striking center; but the central ten-pointed star is surrounded by a pentagon within a series of concentric, sometimes irregular, ovals, the whole forming a disproportionately large figure which runs over the edges and leaves no border. It is possible that his unconventional use of fabric may be a result not of a rejection of the rules but of his sex: perhaps he simply was not aware of the conventions.

6. Utility work, by Theonia Caltas, Salina, Kansas, c. 1940–1960, 68 × 50 inches, appliquéd and pieced knitted wools and cottons. Collection of Ray Wilber and Cathy Dwigans, Baldwin City, Kansas.

Aesthetics were often secondary to utility in the making of a quilt, but most quiltmakers appreciated the chance to exercise their creativity as they cut up old cloth into new designs for quilts to warm their families. Theonia disregarded the convention of disguising the original material in order to create a unified new work of art. In refusing to camouflage the old sweater, she failed to play by the established rules; however, as a Greek immigrant who spoke little English, she may have never fully understood them.

7. *Hexagon*, c. 1940–1950, origin unknown, 78 × 87 inches, pieced cottons and cotton blends, quilted later. Collection of Larry Schwarm, Milwaukee, Wisconsin.

Quilts are bound not only by rules; they are, quite literally, bound by the squared corner. Yet the unknown maker of this quilt rejected the tradition that even a quilt made from hexagonal pieces must become a square or rectangular bedcovering with ninety-degree corner angles. The design repeat led beyond the squared corner, and the quiltmaker followed, finishing a spectacular quilt in a delightful and unconventional manner.

CRAZY QUILT

A STORY BY MARIANNE FONS

My husband thought the situation was caused by poor ventilation. What I mean is, Harold deduced from the available facts that our odd experiences were the result of insufficient oxygen. That's how Harold is—practical, deductive. I can just see his mind at work. First he said to himself, "During the night my wife and I both had extremely odd and uncanny dreams. Undoubtedly, some condition is affecting the atmosphere in the room where we are sleeping, lessening the amount of oxygen available to our brains. Thus, the dreams." Then he would conclude, "A window must be opened." It was, you might say, an open and shut case. Just the thing for Harold, my future lawyer. His mind is like a computer: the facts are fed in, sorted, analyzed, and a rational objective solution is produced.

Now, I'm not like Harold. I get all wrapped up in one detail at a time, forgetting the others until their turns come. I was sitting up in bed, still groggy from my dream. Spread on our bed was the big patchwork quilt, and as I looked at all its colors and patterns and shapes, I knew the quilt itself caused the dreams.

Sunday, the day before, we had gone to a flea market and made one purchase. I saw the quilt at a distance, hanging on a line.

It was not a set pattern, symmetrical, but a crazy quilt, a wild conglomeration of irregular scraps. A whole world seemed to be alive on it. "A Christmas present to ourselves," I thought. I convinced Harold of its quality, its warmth and its value as a collector's item. We carried it home.

The next morning, as I said, I was sitting up in bed, fingering a tiny scrap of brownish velvet. I took a deep breath and said, "No, Harold, there's plenty of oxygen. It's the quilt."

"Oh, Martha!" Harold replied. He was standing before the window, and the morning light put half his face in shadow, but I could read his exasperation. "My dear, I love you," he said, "but the ideas you have utterly astound me."

My theory was simple. The fabrics actually absorbed the lives of those who had worn them. While we were covered by the quilt, the history of those personalities seeped into us. Harold wouldn't buy my view. "Don't let

me forget to open that window tonight," was all he said.

I dropped Harold off at the university where he is a law student and drove on downtown to my job at the bookstore. I was supposed to be rearranging a stock of art books for the pre-Christmas sale. The manager wanted all the coffee-table editions prominently displayed. But I had a hard time keeping my

All photographs by Sharon Risedorph

mind on my work. Last night's dream kept creeping to the surface.

I had dreamed of a night deep in the winter, out in some open country place where the snow was three feet deep on the ground. The sky was clear and the moon was full. I was trying to run through the snow, but I kept falling and getting back up. My body was heavy, and I was

wearing a long, thick nightgown, and was barefoot. Every time I fell, my hair would tangle around my face; as I got up, I would push it back. Even in the dream it seemed strange not to be cold. A farmhouse

was up ahead of me and I was stumbling toward it.

At the bookstore that day, I sat on my little three-legged stool amid the rows of books on Leonardo Da Vinci and Van Gogh and tried to remember the rest of my dream. There had been more, but it was lost, slipped back to wherever dreams go.

That night, Harold remembered to open the window a crack. We both sat up awhile reading. Harold was engrossed in his *Civil Procedures,* and I was nearing the end of *Don Quixote.* I came to the part where Quixote and Sancho are stampeded by a huge herd of pigs, and I just collapsed with laughter. I made him put down his tome; I read him a few paragraphs and got him laughing too. We laughed, and the bed shook. Harold was snoring softly before I dropped off to sleep, and the last thing I remember was stroking the top of the crazy quilt, finding a little patch of silk and wondering whose party dress it had belonged to.

The next morning the alarm rang; Harold thrust his arm out from under the covers and shut it off. He groaned and flopped back against the pillows.

"Nightmare," he said, "perfect nightmare. Shoveling snow...incredible speed... a dozen men."

"A dozen men, Harold?" I asked, "shoveling snow off the road so the horses could pull a wagon through?"

"Yes, yes!" He was confounded. "Exactly, Martha, but how could you know?" He was wide awake, staring at me near-sightedly in the pale light of the morning.

"I was wrapped in blankets in the back of the wagon. Everyone was saying I was mad."

"But that woman was old; she must have weighed two hundred and fifty pounds. She was raving and carrying on. Martha, this is ridiculous. *We can't dream the same dream!*"

But we had. We had dreamed the same thing. As an old woman I had seen the farmhouse through the trees and gone to the window. I knocked on the frost and a lamp was lighted. People peered at me from within and tried to make me come inside, called me Cordelia, then chased and caught me and wrapped me in blankets. They tied my bare feet in rags. I struggled as they put me in the wagon, but I felt calm inside and could hear everything they said. The horses pulled the wagon forward as the men shoveled the way clear.

It took a third night under the quilt before Harold was convinced. The day had worn the edges off the weird, snowy night and, by evening, Harold was sure the window only needed a few inches more. I myself was profoundly interested in the night ahead. I wanted to know where the old woman was going in the wagon.

But I didn't find out. Instead, I found myself in the arms of a man with a silken beard. I snuggled up to Harold and he became a ruddy face, eyes crinkling at the corners, a scimitar of a smile in the moonlight, and warm lips that whispered, "Sarah, oh Sarah, how I love thee." Such a strange, ruddy young man, so real, his broad shoulders and unbuttoned woolly union suit.

Morning came with the light filtering through the sheer curtains of our apartment window. I lay still, with my arms wrapped around my husband, and watched him sleeping. His nostrils moved a little with each breath, and his lips were parted. I studied the details of his face, each curve of bone and flesh. Harold, I thought to myself, are you the man of my dreams?

When he opened his eyes, he seemed not to know me. And then he did, and I knew it had happened again.

Harold found it difficult to accept what had occurred. He kept thinking there had to be a logical explanation, but of course there just wasn't one.

"It's not possible," he said. "It's unnatural. It's supernatural! Nothing like this has ever happened to me before, Martha. I must be going nuts."

I was worried about him. For a person like me, an incident without a normal explanation presents no problem. In fact, I rather like the idea—the mysteries of life and all that. But for Harold it meant a complete breakdown of world order. A raw element had invaded his otherwise well-disciplined mind and threatened him in a truly frightening way. His usually cool brown eyes looked strained behind his glasses. I knew he was tired.

I called in sick at work and Harold stayed home from the university. Classes were out for the holidays and he was just studying anyway. He sat in the rocking chair, wrapped in a terry-cloth bathrobe, and stared at the floor. His sandy hair was tousled and cowlicked in back. He reminded me of a little boy home from school with a cold.

"Want some hot cocoa?" I asked him. I poured the milk into a saucepan and turned on the flame. He kept watching the floor and then burst out laughing.

"Preposterous," he guffawed, "preposterous! I'm letting myself get worked up over nothing. I'm just going to forget about the whole thing. Do me a favor, Love, fold that thing up, wrap it in tissue and put it in the very back of the closet, and let's forget all about it."

"Good idea," I said, humoring him, "forget all about it — brilliant conclusion to a painful case." Harold moved to the table with his cocoa and began spreading out papers and books. He would spend the day at his work after all and wipe out all this foolishness. I smiled at Harold, being so himself.

In the bedroom I tossed the pillows on the floor and began to smooth out the sheets. I pulled the quilt off the bed and gathered up its four corners; as I was folding it, my eye caught an interesting scrap I hadn't noticed before. It was a lovely crescent, like a piece of night, embroidered with stars, around its edges a fancy stitch of white. All the pieces of the quilt were fancy-stitched around the edges, as though each had its own little fence or frame. There were embroidered and painted flowers, animals and birds everywhere, and I sank to the floor, studying scrap after scrap.

The shapes were like people, I thought, like human hearts. As my fingers moved from patch to patch, memories slid by me, of farmhouse rooms, attic cobwebs, beds of childbirth, hay-wagon rides, mattresses on the floor, card-table tents. I had to do some rearranging in the closet to find space for the folded quilt. I pulled out a sack of old clothes for the Salvation Army box.

That evening the light was switched off with a sigh from both of us. I guess it was relief on Harold's part, and on mine too, but I had regrets. I was leaving dozens of dream persons inhospitably cramped in the closet.

We both slept soundly, deeply, right through the alarm, and had to rush like mad to make it to campus and work on time. We didn't have a moment to talk about dreams. Besides, there was nothing to discuss. All I could remember was the ordinary succession of familiar faces in unfamiliar settings, the usual odd combinations of everyday elements, late arrivals at work and buses going backwards. I don't know if Harold dreamed at all.

The bookstore was a madhouse that day, people buying armloads of books for Christmas presents — cookbooks, travel books, children's books, best sellers, everyone wanting boxes and gift wrapping. It was almost six by the time we got the money counted and locked up the store. The car lights and freeway lights gave me a cozy, Christmasy feeling. I thought about getting a tree, but I knew Harold would say it was entirely too early. He insists that if you get one too soon it's dry as a bone by Christmas, no matter what you do.

He wasn't on his accustomed bench when I got to the university, so I assumed he had caught a bus when I was late. The apartment was dark, but I could hear him snoring the moment I let myself in. I switched on a couple of lights and then looked in the bedroom. I couldn't believe what I saw. There was Harold, sprawled face down on the bed, wrapped in the crazy quilt.

I shook his shoulder gently. "Harold, wake up," I said, "are you all right?" He mumbled and groaned, and at first I couldn't make out what he was saying.

"Horse...beautiful horse...ran like the wind...won the race."

Gradually I got the whole story out of him. He hadn't been able to concentrate on his studies, couldn't work in the library, and at noon walked out to the street and caught a bus.

"I rode through the city," he said, "just feeling restless. The minute I got home I went straight to the closet and unwrapped it." His eyes sparkled as he patted the quilt. He had a marvelous dream about a race track and thoroughbred horses, a beautiful bay he had ridden first across the finish line.

While I fried the hamburgers, Harold made a salad, or tried to. He was so excited about the horse race that he kept forgetting completely what he was doing. He recalled every detail of the course, the pastel colors of his silks and the angle of the riding crop, with its small tassel at the tip.

"It was so thrilling, Martha, so real. I feel as though I were really there."

We ate in silence, Harold lost in reverie, my own mind dazed and unbelieving. Only a day or so ago, Harold said he thought he was going nuts, and I hadn't taken him seriously. As I sat across from him at the table and watched the strange light in his eyes, I thought he might be right. When he got up yawning and said he thought he'd turn in early, I knew something was definitely wrong. When he stayed home from the university again the next day, I knew something had to be done.

I thought bitterly of all Harold's plans for this vacation, how he was going to "utilize the time to the utmost," as he put it, studying next semester's material and catching up on all the little things that needed to be done, writing letters and doing bookkeeping. What a joke that turned out to be! Instead, he was spending all his time snoring under that blasted quilt. If it hadn't been Christmas vacation, Harold's future as a lawyer would be going down the drain.

I bought a little Christmas tree on my

way home that evening. He watched as I set it up. I had hoped the lights and decorations and my small collection of packages might snap him back into the real world, but he just stared at the little glass candles, the liquid bubbles reflected in his eyes, and said nothing.

I began that night to cut little pieces out of the quilt with my fingernail scissors. I knelt by the bed while Harold slept softly and, with the utmost care, I snipped the embroidery thread, loosened each patch, removed it and placed it in an envelope. It was midnight by the time I had removed just six pieces. I leaned my head down on the bed and tried to think, but soon I was sleeping and dreaming too, my face against the quilt. This time I saw rows and rows of growing vegetables. I was standing among them in a cotton dress, holding a hoe. Above me was an azure sky with friendly white clouds. A little tow-headed child held my hem and cried.

The next morning I awoke stiff and disoriented. No alarm had been set, but I had time to change clothes and get to work. I drove down the street, thinking about my still-sleeping husband, the patchwork quilt and myself.

Buying the quilt had been my idea. I was the one who knew right away that the quilt was responsible for the crazy dreams. I'm the one who is supposed to love mystery and magic. I've always said Harold was too studious, too conscientious, too dull, that he should open up a little and accept some strangeness in the world. I felt ashamed for what I had done to the quilt. It was an awful day all the way around. I was tired and preoccupied. I'm sure my customers figured I was a typically inept Christmas extra. As closing time came, I knew I would be up late again that night, putting the patches back.

But when I got home, Harold was in the rocking chair waiting for me, the inevitable crazy quilt draped across his knees. His robe was rumpled, his unopened books were on the table, and dirty dishes were everywhere. He had a sad, sleepy expression on his face, and he just looked at me while I put my purse down and got my coat off. Then he folded back a corner of the quilt to show the place I had scalped. How he must have studied that wild field of colors to have noticed my hand-sized crime!

"How could you, Martha?" he asked. "How could you do this?"

I got out my sewing box and the scraps I had cut off. I brought a lamp and chair over beside Harold and went to work, doing my best to resew the pieces just as they had been, not really knowing how. I stitched around one and then another of the scraps, saying nothing. Harold watched me as I labored and, after an hour or so, I sensed a change in him, though he was silent too. It was as if he began thinking for himself again, as though he were no longer dreaming.

I saw I was coming out short of cloth. I had folded back too much fabric, I guess. I had not been able to make the fancy embroidery stitches to join the pieces. Harold got up and brought over the sack set aside for the Salvation Army box. He pulled out an old shirt of his and a blouse of mine. Together we cut and trimmed two extra patches to complete the mending of the crazy quilt.

"Let's give it away," he said. "Let's give it to someone for Christmas." My mind ran dully through the members of our families.

"I mean," he said, "let's just go walking and find someone out in the world to give it to."

I was slow putting on my coat while he practically jumped into his jeans and sweater. We gathered up the quilt and went outside. The air was cold as we walked down the sidewalk. Windows in all the old brick apartment houses were cheerily lighted up, squares and rectangles and occasional ovals of warmth, some with Advent candles on the sills or holly wreaths hanging from the sashes, all shining out in a fabric of night.

We came to the nearest busy street and turned by the corner grocery. Half of the little parking lot was filled with Christmas trees; the scent of evergreen reached us before we even saw them. There was an archway between the first two rows, and a sign overhead that read "Odd Fellows Lodge No. 81." Through the archway I could see the alley where a small trailer was parked for an office, and just to the side of it a bonfire was crackling on the pavement, consuming the scraps of evergreen and fallen pine needles.

A little old man was dozing in the doorway of the trailer, asleep with his head against the jamb. His jacket was buttoned up to the neck, his short arms were folded on his chest, and

his booted legs were crossed on the steps in front of him.

He did not awaken as we tucked the quilt around him. His features seemed to change just slightly as the warmth of it enveloped him, and a smile played at the corner of his mouth. I think he began to dream at once.

MARIANNE FONS is a quiltmaker who lives in the country near Winterset, Iowa. In addition to pursuing her interests in needlework and writing, she teaches and lectures throughout the United States. She is author, with Liz Porter, of *Classic Quilted Vests* and *Classic Basket Patterns*, both published by Yours Truly, Inc.

Illustrating this article is *Crazy*, by Katherine Wells Codding, Duluth, Minnesota, 1885, 62 × 62 inches, silks and velvets. Collection of Charles and Alta Codding, Bowling Green, Ohio.

Other Books from
THE QUILT

COMING IN SEPTEMBER 1985

Remember Me: *Women & Their Friendship Quilts* by Linda Otto Lipsett. Our readers praised Linda's remarkable article, "A Piece of Ellen's Dress," in *The Quilt Digest 2*. Now, she returns with a full-length book. In *Remember Me*, combining painstakingly-gathered research with a deep, abiding understanding of her subjects, Linda lovingly recreates the lives of several nineteenth-century quiltmakers, their families and friends.

This is a book about beautiful friendship quilts, and much more. It tells the true stories of women, their joys and sorrows, loves and devotions. These remarkable histories will transport you back into the nineteenth century. This is a book that will educate, entertain and inspire.

In August, advance information will be sent to persons whose names are on our mailing list.

$16.95
96 pages
71 color photographs

Homage to Amanda. This is an informative full-color chronicle of the American quilt, as exemplified by an extraordinary collection. Two of America's most noted collectors, Edwin Binney, 3rd and his daughter, quiltmaker Gail Binney-Winslow, thoroughly discuss their quilt collection, showing how it represents the development of American quiltmaking from the eighteenth century to the present day. Available now.

DIGEST PRESS

The Quilt Digest 2. Articles include "A Piece of Ellen's Dress" by Linda Lipsett; "The Collector: Looking Toward the Future" by Michael Kile; "Victorian Style: Vintage Photographs of an American Home," sepia-tone views of a turn-of-the-century Chicago home, complete with crazy quilts, with an introduction by Penny McMorris; "The Collector's Guide for the Care of Quilts in the Home," by Patsy Orlofsky; "Ku'u Hae Aloha," new discoveries about the Royal Hawaiian Flag quilt, by Elizabeth Akana; and "Showcase," displaying twenty-three fine antique and contemporary quilts in full color, compiled by Roderick Kiracofe. The second in our annual series.

$12.95
80 pages • 60 color photographs
17 black-and-white photographs and illustrations

$12.95
70 pages
48 color photographs
19 black-and-white photographs

The Quilt Digest 1. Articles include "The Log Cabin: An American Quilt on the Western Frontier" by Sandi Fox; "Amish Interiors," an essay by David Pottinger, accompanied by black-and-white photographs of the inside of Amish homes by Susan Einstein; "Surviving without Selling Out: Thoughts from a Quilt Artist's Journal" by Michael James; "The Reiter Quilt: A Family Story in Cloth," the odyssey of a Jewish immigrant and her remarkable quilt, as told by Julie Silber; "The Collector: Free Spirit in the West," a look at this country's most extensive gathering of Amish quilts, by Michael Kile; "Collecting Quilt Data: History from Statistics" by Jonathan Holstein; and "Showcase," a full-color display of twenty remarkable contemporary and antique quilts, compiled by Roderick Kiracofe. Our first volume, already a collector's item.

Thousands of quilt, antique, book and museum shops around the world carry the books we publish. Check with shops in your area. Or you may order books directly from us.

To order, send us your name, address, city, state and zip code. Tell us which books you wish to order and in what quantity. California residents add 6% sales tax. Finally, to the price of the books you order, add $1.50 for the first book and $1.00 for each additional book to cover postage and handling charges. Enclose your check made payable to *The Quilt Digest Press* and mail it, along with the above information, to Dept. D, 955 Fourteenth Street, San Francisco 94114.

Readers outside the United States may have their orders shipped via air mail by including $6.00 for each book ordered. All orders from outside the United States must be accompanied by payment in U.S. dollars drawn on a U.S. bank.

Depending upon the season of the year, allow 4–6 weeks for delivery. Readers outside the United States should allow several additional weeks for sea delivery.

We are happy to send gift books directly to recipients.

Wholesale information is available upon request.

OUR MAILING LIST

If your name is not on our mailing list and you would like it to be, please write to us. We will be happy to add your name so that you will receive advance information about our forthcoming books.

NEWS ABOUT THE QUILT DIGEST 4

We are already at work on this exciting volume. Leading quilt experts have been commissioned to write the articles. You can expect the same high-quality design and finely-reproduced color photographs you enjoy in all our books.

Available in April 1986.